W9-ACY-060

The Large Print Roget's II Thesaurus

Houghton Mifflin Company
Boston New York

This Large Print Book carries the Seal of Approval of N. A.V. H.

Library of Congress Cataloging-in-Publication Data
Roget's II
The large print Roget's II thesaurus.
p. cm.
ISBN 0-395-92933-4
1. Large type books. 2. English language — Synonyms and antonyms. I. Houghton Mifflin Company. II. Title.
[PE1591.R715 1998]
423'.1 — dc21 98-8701
CIP

Manufactured in the United States of America

ABCDEFG-DOC-998

CONTENTS

HOW TO USE THIS BOOK

Roget's is a unique thesaurus. Unlike a traditional thesaurus that prints exhaustive undifferentiated synonym lists, *Roget's* provides synonym studies on the most important meanings and ideas and discriminates among many of the most frequently used—and misused—words in the English language. Whether you are looking for the precise word to express a specific thought or only for a synonym to express a simple thought, you will find that *Roget's* is the handiest and most practical thesaurus available for the office or classroom.

What is a Synonym?

Synonyms are words that are the same or nearly the same in meaning. Although all the synonyms entered in the individual lists in this thesaurus share an important aspect of meaning, there are often differences in shades of meaning. For example, consider *clean* and its synonyms *cleanly*, *immaculate*, and *spotless*. Basically all four words have the same meaning: they describe what is free from dirt, stains, or impurities. *Clean* is the most general word. *Immaculate* and *spotless* usually refer to what is ''perfectly clean,'' but *immaculate* is a more formal term and *spotless* a more conversational one. *Cleanly*, on the other hand, is most often used to describe what is ''habitually neat and clean.''

Synonym Studies

Roget's contains two kinds of synonym studies: relatively long paragraphs that discuss the synonyms in detail and short studies that focus on one central meaning of a number of common terms. These studies are organized alphabetically and present the synonyms in the following format: the entry word is given in boldface, followed by a part of speech (*adj.*, adjective; *adv.*, adverb; *n.*, noun; and *v.*, verb) and by the word's synonyms:

relevant ***adj.*** **germane, material, pertinent.**

Discriminated Synonymies. The foundation of *Roget's* is a block of synonym paragraphs in which the meaning shared by all the words is supplemented by additional material that discriminates the various shades of meaning of each word:

> **relevant** ***adj.*** **germane, material, pertinent.** RELEVANT and its synonyms describe what is associated with a matter or situation at hand and has direct bearing on it: *Stick to relevant questions, please!* PERTINENT implies a logical and precise bearing: *The pertinent statistics do not confirm the press accounts of the accident.* GERMANE applies to what is so closely akin to the subject as to reinforce it: *statements germane to the topic of his speech.* MATERIAL has the sense of being needed to complete a subject: *material evidence.*

Antonyms—words that are opposite in meaning—are given at the end of many of the discriminated paragraphs. Not all antonyms given at a synonym study are themselves main entries. For example:

bare . . .
Antonym: **covered.**

Many words or senses of words have no true antonyms. For instance, the opposite of the verb *change* is best expressed by saying "to remain unchanged."

On the other hand, some words have more than one antonym:

generous . . .
Antonyms: **cheap; stingy.**

Such listings alert you to the fact that various shades of meaning are covered by the antonyms given.

It should be emphasized that antonyms apply only to the entry words; they may apply to some of the synonyms, but often they do not.

Core-meaning synonymies. Interspersed with the discriminated synonymies are core-meaning studies that focus on a basic meaning shared by all the synonyms. In these the synonym list is followed by a definition and one or more examples using the main-entry word:

> **surpass** *v.* **exceed, excel, outdo, outshine, outstrip, pass, top, transcend.** *Core meaning:* To be greater or better than (*a wheat crop that surpassed last year's by two million bushels*).

Note that any of the other synonyms in the list can be substituted for *surpass* in the illustrative example.

Some of the core-meaning studies treat different forms of words that are dealt with in the discriminated studies and do not require additional discussion (such as *fair* and *fairly*). Most of these studies, however, deal with simple concepts; they offer an ample choice of synonyms for the most frequently used words—those words for which a person seeks an alternative to bring variety to his or her writing.

> **executive** *adj.* **administrative, managerial.** *Core meaning:* Of, for, or relating to administration (*an executive secretary; an executive committee*).

A–Z WORD LIST

abandon *v.* **desert, forsake, leave, quit.**
Core meaning: To give up without intending to return or claim again (*abandoned his family*).

abandoned *adj.* **derelict, deserted, forlorn, forsaken.**
Core meaning: Having been given up or left alone (*an abandoned house; an abandoned strategy*).

aberrant See **abnormal.**

abeyance *n.* **dormancy, latency, quiescence, remission, suspension.**
Core meaning: The condition of being temporarily inactive (*hold a decision in abeyance*).

abhor See **hate.**

abhorrence See **hate.**

ability *n.* **1. capacity, skill, talent.**
These words name qualities that enable one to do something desirable and usually rather difficult. ABILITY stresses the fact or power of accomplishment (*a person of great musical ability*), and CAPACITY the potential for such accomplishment (*a capacity for learning*). TALENT is usually regarded as a natural gift for achievement in a specific area: *artistic talent*. SKILL often implies proven expertness in an art or trade requiring practical, specialized knowledge: *skill in carpentry*.
2. See **expertise.**

able *adj.* **capable, competent, qualified.**
ABLE when it follows a verb like *be* or *feel* implies the capacity to serve in a given function but does not suggest any particular standard of performance: *He was able to ski*. When *able* precedes a noun, however, it indicates more than usual ability, skill, etc.: *an able skier*. CAPABLE implies the ability to meet usual required standards: *a capable teacher*. COMPETENT implies workmanlike standards: *a competent typist*. QUALIFIED connotes compliance with set standards of training or experience: *a qualified physician*.

abnormal ***adj.*** **aberrant, atypical, irregular.**
All of these refer to what deviates from a usual pattern, level, or type. ABNORMAL often suggests that something is strange (*an abnormal interest in bats*) or unhealthy (*an abnormal temperature*). ABERRANT and ATYPICAL both describe what differs from the normal or typical, but *aberrant* is the stronger term and sometimes even suggests a lapse in mental faculties: *aberrant behavior; an atypical response.* IRREGULAR has wide application; it can refer to what is not uniform, as in shape (*an irregular coastline*), does not follow a set pattern (*irregular rhythm*), or is unusual or improper (*a highly irregular procedure*).
Antonym: **normal.**

abolish ***v.*** **eradicate, exterminate, extinguish, extirpate, obliterate.**
These verbs mean to put an end to. ABOLISH is most often related to banning or outlawing existing conditions or regulations: *abolished Prohibition; abolish poll taxes.* EXTERMINATE refers to destruction of living things by deliberate, selective means: *exterminate rats.* To EXTINGUISH is to put out—a fire, for example, or something likened to a flame, such as human life or hope. ERADICATE and EXTIRPATE refer to extermination or to destruction of the whole of nonliving objects, as by rooting up or out; both imply wiping out by removing all trace, a sense that OBLITERATE makes more explicitly: *villages obliterated by bombing.* See also **destroy.**

abominable See **unspeakable.**

aboriginal See **native.**

about See **approximately.**

absence ***n.*** **nonappearance, nonattendance.**
Core meaning: Failure to be present (*everyone at the meeting noticed her absence*).

absolute ***adj.*** **despotic, totalitarian, tyrannical.**
Core meaning: Having supreme, unlimited power and control (*an absolute ruler*).

absolve See **vindicate.**

absorb *v.* **assimilate, digest, imbibe.**
Core meaning: To take in and incorporate (*quickly absorbs new ideas*).

abstain See **refrain.**

abstinence ***n.*** **continence, sobriety, temperance.**
These nouns denote self-denial or self-restraint in the gratification of human appetites. ABSTINENCE is most often applied to voluntary refraining from food and drink considered harmful. CONTINENCE usually refers to self-denial in sexual activity. SOBRIETY is the absence of alcoholic intoxication. TEMPERANCE can mean complete refraining from alcoholic drink but more often denotes moderation in drinking.

abstract See **theoretical.**

abstruse See **ambiguous.**

absurd ***adj.*** **ludicrous, preposterous, ridiculous.**
These words all describe what obviously lacks sense or departs from logic. ABSURD is the most general: *an absurd suggestion.* PREPOSTEROUS is more intense than *absurd* and describes what is completely unreasonable: *a preposterous story.* LUDICROUS and RIDICULOUS often apply to absurdities that inspire laughter; *ridiculous* implies mockery: *a ludicrous costume; a ridiculous idea.*
Antonym: **sensible.**

abuse *v.* **maltreat, mistreat, misuse.**
ABUSE and its synonyms mean to treat or use wrongly. *Abuse* most often expresses action, by deed or word, that is harmful to persons; the injury may be calculated and malicious or may result from overindulgence in such things as alcohol, drugs, or a privilege: *abused his eyesight by reading in poor light; a child who had been abused by its parents.* MISUSE is generally applied to improper use of things resulting from ignorance or oversight: *misuse our natural resources.* MISTREAT and MALTREAT both imply rough handling, usually of persons or animals, that causes physical

injury; *maltreat* especially suggests deliberate cruelty: *an angry man who mistreated his son by boxing his ears; maltreating the dog by pulling his tail.*

abusive ***adj.*** **contumelious, invective, opprobrious, reviling, scurrilous, vituperative.**
Core meaning: Of, related to, or characterized by verbal abuse (*abusive remarks*).

academic See **theoretical.**

accelerate See **expedite.**

accept ***v.*** **1. embrace, take up, welcome.**
Core meaning: To receive something offered willingly and gladly (*accepted the award*).
2. admit, receive, take in.
Core meaning: To allow admittance (*accepted for membership in the club*).
3. See **believe.**

accessible See **convenient.**

accidental ***adj.*** **chance, fortuitous, haphazard, random.**
All of these words describe what is unexpected or unplanned. What is ACCIDENTAL happens unintentionally: *an accidental mistake.* CHANCE and FORTUITOUS imply lack of cause or design: *a chance* (or *fortuitous*) *meeting.* HAPHAZARD and RANDOM suggest the absence of patterns of selection or order: *a haphazard* (or *random*) *collection.*
Antonym: **intentional.**

acclaim See **praise.**

accompany ***v.*** **chaperon, conduct, escort.**
These verbs mean to be with or go with another. ACCOMPANY implies being or going on an equal footing with the other person or persons: *accompanied her friend on a trip to Europe.* CONDUCT stresses guidance of the other or others: *conducting a tour of the city.* ESCORT suggests either protective guidance (*police escorting the President during the parade*) or observance of social forms (*Jack escorted Mrs. Clark to the concert*). CHAPERON (or *chaperone*)

specifies protective accompaniment, usually of a young person by an adult: *chaperoned her friend's daughter during her travels.*

accomplice See **partner.**

accomplish See **reach.**

accord See **harmony.**

accountable See **liable.**

accredit See **attribute.**

accumulate See **gather.**

accuracy See **veracity.**

accurate See **true.**

accuse *v.* **arraign, charge, impeach, indict.**
These words share the general sense "to blame someone for a fault, error, or offense." ACCUSE and CHARGE are the most general and can be used in both legal and personal contexts. ARRAIGN, IMPEACH, and INDICT apply to formal legal procedure. To *arraign* is to call a prisoner before a court to answer an indictment; *impeach,* to charge with misconduct in office before a proper court of justice; and *indict*, to make a formal accusation against on the basis of the findings of a jury, especially a grand jury.
Antonym: **vindicate.**

achieve See **reach.**

acknowledge *v.* **admit, concede, confess, own.**
ACKNOWLEDGE and its synonyms refer to making a statement that grants the truth of something at issue. *Acknowledge* expresses that basic sense with fewer overtones than the other words. ADMIT more strongly implies reluctance to grant such a truth because the truth is to one's disadvantage: *admit a mistake*. CONCEDE also suggests a disadvantageous statement resulting from yielding under the pressure of contrary evidence: *conceded that his data were inconclusive*. CONFESS can be the mere equivalent of *admit* or *concede* but more strictly applies to formal disclosure of

wrongdoing: *confessed her crime* (or *her sins*). OWN also can have the force of *admit* or *concede* (*I own that I've made a mistake*), but in the combination *own up* it means to confess fully and openly: *owned up to a long record of falsehood.*

acme See **climax.**

acquit See **vindicate.**

active ***adj.*** **busy, dynamic, energetic, lively, vigorous.**
These mean taking part in some action or activity. ACTIVE suggests contribution: *an active member of the club.* BUSY implies sustained activity, without regard for its quality or worth: *busy playing cards.* DYNAMIC suggests forcefulness and intensity (*a dynamic salesman*); ENERGETIC, enthusiasm and unflagging strength (*an energetic campaigner*). LIVELY applies to what is full of life (*a lively baby*); VIGOROUS adds the implication of healthy strength: *a vigorous sportsman.*
Antonym: **inactive.**

actually ***adv.*** **genuinely, indeed, really.**
Core meaning: In point of fact (*He said he was studying when actually he was at the movies*).

acute 1. See **critical. 2.** See **sharp.**

add ***v.*** **figure, sum (up), tally, total.**
Core meaning: To combine figures to form a sum (*adding the day's receipts*).

address See **send.**

adequate See **sufficient.**

adhere See **bond.**

ad-lib See **improvise.**

administer ***v.*** **administrate, direct, govern, head, manage, run, superintend.**
Core meaning: To have charge of the affairs of others (*administer a colony*).

administrate See **administer.**

administrative See **executive.**

admit 1. See **acknowledge. 2.** See **accept.**

admonish *v.* **rebuke, reprimand, reproach, reprove.** These verbs mean to address someone disapprovingly in consequence of the person's fault or misdeed. ADMONISH refers to mild criticism (*admonished them for being late*); in a related sense the word means to counsel against—to warn as a means of rectifying or avoiding error (*admonished us to be careful*). REPROVE implies more pronounced disapproval, as does REPROACH, which often also suggests a feeling of injury and disappointment over another's conduct. REBUKE refers to sharp criticism, and REPRIMAND to severe criticism that is often a formal or official expression of disapproval by one in authority.

admonishment See **warning.**

admonition See **warning.**

adolescent See **young.**

adopt See **borrow.**

adore See **love.**

adroit See **graceful.**

adult See **mature.**

advance *v.* **1. proceed, progress.** ADVANCE, PROCEED, and PROGRESS share the meaning of moving forward, literally or figuratively. *Advance* is often restricted to certain constructions, as: *The troops advanced at a rapid pace. He advanced a step. The editors advanced the deadline by two months. Proceed* emphasizes continuing motion: *She proceeded toward Boston by Route 2. Progress* suggests steady improvement or development: *His music studies progressed satisfactorily.*
Antonym: **recede.**
2. further, promote.
These verbs share the meaning of assisting in making something—such as a cause or a business venture—go forward: *Scientific and medical research advance knowledge.* PROMOTE and FURTHER in particular stress active support and

encouragement: *a campaign to promote a new product; promote a corporal to sergeant; furthering his career by attending classes at night school.*
Antonym: **hinder.**

adversary See **opponent.**

adverse See **unfavorable.**

advertise ***or*** **advertize 1.** ***v.*** **broadcast, disseminate, promulgate.**
Core meaning: To make information generally known (*advertised her engagement by wearing a diamond*).
2. build up, plug (*Informal*), **promote, publicize, push.**
Core meaning: to make known the positive features of a product (*advertise a new computer*).

affable See **amiable.**

affect ***v.*** **impress, influence, move, strike, touch.**
These verbs mean to produce a mental or emotional effect or response. AFFECT, TOUCH, and MOVE refer to arousing of emotions. *Affect* is nonspecific; *touch* implies a momentary sense of pity or tenderness (*a kindness that touched her*), and *move* a profound feeling capable of producing action: *a sight that moved them more than words*. What STRIKES one causes an immediate, abrupt mental response: *struck by her boldness*. What IMPRESSES has a marked, lasting effect, often favorable: *impressed the danger on us; impressed by her lack of fear*. What INFLUENCES produces a mental effect that controls a corresponding response: *influenced his decision to resign*.

affectation ***n.*** **air, airs, mannerism, pose.**
These are forms of human behavior that are often artificial and may serve to provide a false claim to distinction. AFFECTATION and POSE always denote something not true to one's nature. A mode of dress and a habit of speech can be examples of *affectation,* which applies to a particular trait. A *pose* is a series of such artificial devices or an attitude that may seek to mask one's unworthy nature or merely promote a notion of superiority. A MANNERISM is a distinctive

trait or idiosyncrasy, not necessarily false, that may strike another as distracting or foolish. An AIR is the sum of traits that contribute to an impressive personal bearing or manner, not necessarily false: *an air of mystery about him.* AIRS, however, always refers to an offensive and dubious claim to superiority: *putting on airs.*

affecting See **moving.**

affection See **love.**

affirm See **assert.**

affix See **attach.**

afflict *v.* **agonize, curse, plague, rack, scourge, torment, torture.**
Core meaning: To bring great harm or suffering to (*afflicted with chronic back problems*).

affluent See **rich.**

affront See **offend.**

after See **later.**

age *n.* **day(s), epoch, era, period, time(s).**
Core meaning: A particular time notable for its distinctive characteristics (*the Victorian age*).

aged See **old.**

agency See **means.**

agenda See **program.**

aggravate See **annoy.**

agonize See **afflict.**

agony See **distress.**

agree *v.* **coincide, conform, correspond.**
AGREE and its synonyms express compatibility between people or things. *Agree* may simply indicate freedom from difference or conflict (*His sisters agreed on the choice of his Christmas gift*), but it often suggests arriving at a settlement, and thus accommodation: *Management agreed to raise wages.* COINCIDE stresses exact agreement in space,

time, or thought: *The geometric figures coincided. Our political opinions coincide.* CONFORM stresses close resemblance, sometimes because of adjustment to established standards: *His behavior conformed with the family's wishes. He conformed his behavior to please his family.* CORRESPOND refers to similarity in form or nature or to similarity in function of dissimilar things: *Our ideas do not correspond. A modern stove corresponds to a sixteenth-century fireplace.*
Antonym: **disagree.**

agreeable 1. See **amiable. 2.** See **pleasant.**

aid See **help.**

air See **affectation.**

airs See **affectation.**

alarm See **frighten.**

alert ***adj.*** **1. observant, open-eyed, vigilant, wary, watchful.**
Core meaning: Vigilantly attentive (*alert to danger*).
2. See **clever.**

alien See **foreign.**

alienate See **estrange.**

alive ***adj.*** **live, living.**
These words all describe what has life or continuing existence: *Is the tree still alive? The victory kept their hopes alive. We saw a real live lizard. Drug abuse is a live topic. The living relatives all attended the funeral. The monument on his tomb is a living reminder of his achievements.*
Antonym: **dead.**

allege See **assert.**

all-out See **utter.**

allow See **permit.**

allowance See **permission.**

allure See **seduce.**

ally See **partner.**

almost See **approximately.**

alone *adj.* **lone, lonely, lonesome, solitary.**
These are applied to what is apart from others. ALONE describes such a condition in a manner that can range from matter-of-fact to very emphatic: *alone in her office; alone in the world.* LONE and SOLITARY stress singleness or lack of companionship: *a lone* (or *solitary*) *figure. Solitary* also can emphasize physical isolation or seclusion: *solitary confinement; a solitary nook.* LONELY and, less often, LONESOME are emphatic terms for describing isolation or the absence of others: *a lonely existence; that lonesome road.* More often they indicate a person's sense of dejection arising from general lack of companionship or the absence of specific companions: *a lonely boy; lonesome for old friends.*

aloneness *n.* **isolation, loneliness, loneness, solitude.**
Core meaning: The quality or state of being alone (*Aloneness often causes depression*).

alter See **change.**

alternative See **choice.**

amass See **gather.**

amateur *n.* **dilettante.**
An AMATEUR engages in an art, a science, or a sport for enjoyment rather than for money: *an orchestra made up of amateurs.* The word may imply a lack of professional skill: *a rambling novel written by an amateur.* A DILETTANTE is a person who has taken up an interest in an art or another branch of knowledge for amusement or pleasure; the interest is often merely superficial: *a dilettante in painting.*
Antonym: **professional.**

amazing See **fabulous.**

ambiguous *adj.* **abstruse, cryptic, enigmatic, equivocal, obscure, recondite, vague.**
These describe what is difficult to understand. AMBIGUOUS applies to what can be interpreted in several ways, usually because of faulty expression: *ambiguous directions.* EQUIV-

OCAL strongly implies that such multiple interpretation results from a deliberate attempt to evade, hedge, or cloud a matter at issue: *an equivocal reply*. Something VAGUE lacks clarity of form, owing to poor expression or fuzzy thought. Something OBSCURE is so little known that its meaning seems hardly worth investigating: *obscure legal details*. RECONDITE refers to what is deeply learned and beyond average understanding: *recondite scholarly pursuits*. To that sense ABSTRUSE adds the suggestion of complex expression. CRYPTIC and ENIGMATIC imply the tantalizing character of a riddle, whose meaning lies hidden under an inscrutable or misleading exterior: *a cryptic remark; an enigmatic smile*.

ambition ***n.*** **drive, enterprise, initiative, push** (*Informal*).
Core meaning: The wish or ability to begin and follow through with a plan or task (*a woman of great energy and ambition*).

ambush ***v.*** **bushwhack, surprise, waylay.**
Core meaning: To attack suddenly and without warning (*muggers ambushed them in the park*).

amend See **correct.**

amiable ***adj.*** **affable, agreeable, good-natured, obliging.**
These describe the dispositions and behavior of persons showing a tendency to please in social relations. AMIABLE suggests those qualities opposed to enmity, such as evenness of temper and sweetness of nature. AFFABLE describes one who is mild-mannered and pleasant, and GOOD-NATURED one who is easygoing and tolerant. AGREEABLE implies readiness to please others and comply with their wishes. OBLIGING suggests politeness and readiness to do favors.

amicable See **friendly.**

amid See **among.**

amiss See **awry.**

among ***prep.*** **amid, between.**
AMONG, AMID, and BETWEEN all indicate a middle or intermediate position in space, but in that sense are carefully

distinguished in usage. *Among* and *amid* (or *in the midst of*) connote a position in the company of other persons or things and usually also the state of being surrounded by them. *Among* implies that the persons or things are capable of being construed individually, as separable entities: *circulated among the delegates; gold nuggets among the pebbles*. *Amid* is sometimes used in the same way (*a nest amid the branches*), but the things surrounding or enveloping are often a collective mass rather than separable units: *poverty amid plenty*. *Between* indicates an intermediate location in the space separating two people, places, or things: *a stop between Pittsburgh and Philadelphia*.

amplitude See **bulk.**

amuse ***v.*** **divert, entertain.**
AMUSE and its synonyms refer to actions that provide pleasure, especially as a means of spending leisure time. *Amuse* is the least specific when it refers to something done by and for oneself. DIVERT implies distraction from worry or care. ENTERTAIN suggests something done for others and thus often implies a certain degree of formality.
Antonym: **bore.**

amusement See **recreation.**

analysis ***n.*** **1. breakdown, dissection, resolution.**
Core meaning: The separation of a whole into its parts for study (*a harmonic analysis of a Bach fugue*).
2. examination, inspection, investigation, review, survey.
Core meaning: A close or systematic study (*an analysis of voting trends*).

ancestor ***n.*** **forebear, forefather, progenitor.**
These are all words for any person from whom one is descended directly, especially if that person is of a generation earlier than a grandparent.
Antonym: **descendant.**

ancient See **old.**

anger ***n.*** **fury, indignation, ire, rage, resentment, wrath.**
These name emotional states that may result when one is

greatly displeased. ANGER is the general term overlapping the others. RESENTMENT, which is ill will caused by a sense of being wronged or offended, most often suggests smoldering anger, whereas INDIGNATION implies overt display of grievance over injustice, meanness, or the like. RAGE is violent anger, as is FURY, which suggests even more strongly a wild, uncontrolled display. IRE, a literary term, and WRATH are approximately equivalent in suggesting extreme resentment that seeks expression as revenge or retribution.

anguish See **sorrow.**

animosity See **enmity.**

animus See **enmity.**

annoy *v.* **aggravate, bother, irk, irritate, peeve, provoke, rile, vex.**
ANNOY and its synonyms express the action of disturbing persons by causing mental discomfort of varying intensity. *Annoy* usually refers to minor disturbance. BOTHER suggests mild discomfort resulting from the imposition of a nuisance, and PEEVE a disturbance that produces a mildly resentful response. IRK implies imposition that wearies one. VEX often suggests repeated, petty impositions; sometimes it adds the related sense of confusing or baffling. IRRITATE applies to a stronger disturbance and angry response, as do PROVOKE and AGGRAVATE (informal in this sense); all suggest a taxing of patience, and *provoke* especially implies deliberate imposition. RILE refers to the stirring of strong anger, openly expressed. See also **displease.**

annul See **cancel.**

answer *v.* **reply, respond, retort.**
These refer to speaking or otherwise acting as a consequence of another's speech or act. ANSWER and REPLY, the most general, can refer to both language and action such as gesturing or bodily movement, but most often are applied to speech that follows a single direct question. When what follows is written, *reply* is the more common. RESPOND can

refer to spoken or written language; of all these words, it is in widest use to indicate an act or action that follows a stimulus of the kind noted, and in one sense it means to react in a particular or desired way: *respond to affection.* RETORT is largely limited to what is spoken—to a quick, direct statement sometimes noteworthy for wit, style of expression, etc.

answerable See **liable.**

antagonism See **enmity.**

antagonist See **opponent.**

antagonistic See **unfriendly.**

anticipate See **foresee.**

antipathy See **enmity.**

antique See **old.**

anxiety ***n.*** **care, concern, worry.**

These nouns express troubled states of mind. ANXIETY indicates a feeling of fear and apprehension, especially when what causes the feeling is unidentifiable: *anxiety about taking a plane.* CARE implies mental distress caused by heavy responsibilities: *the cares involved in raising a large family.* CONCERN stresses personal involvement in the source of mental unrest; it has more to do with serious thought than with emotion: *The doctor's gentle concern helped the patient recover.* WORRY implies persistent doubt or fear that disturbs one's peace of mind: *Business worries ruined her evening.*

Antonym: **tranquillity.**

apathetic ***adj.*** **disinterested, indifferent, insensible, lethargic, listless.**

Core meaning: Without emotion or interest (*apathetic voters*).

apathy See **disinterest.**

apex See **climax.**

apogee See **climax.**

appear *v.* **look, seem.**
Core meaning: To have the appearance of (*He appeared happy but really wasn't*).

appease See **pacify.**

appellation See **name.**

appendage See **branch.**

appreciable See **perceptible.**

appreciate *v.* **cherish, prize, treasure, value.**
All of these verbs express a favorable opinion of someone or something. APPRECIATE applies especially when high regard is based on critical assessment and judgment: *Many people appreciate the paintings of Renoir.* More loosely, it implies a sense of gratitude or warm response: *We appreciate your kindness to our parents.* CHERISH and TREASURE usually suggest affectionate regard: *She cherished her grandmother's teapot. Mr. Hubbard treasures his vintage Rolls Royce.* PRIZE emphasizes pride of possession: *She prized her collection of antiques.* The connotations of VALUE may range from mild appreciation or regard (*I value his opinion*) to what is rated above all else (*Ancient Romans often valued their honor more than life*).
Antonym: **despise.**

apprehend 1. See **arrest. 2.** See **comprehend.**

approach *n.* **advent, coming, convergence, imminence, nearness.**
Core meaning: The act or fact of coming near (*the advent of a new computer era*).

appropriate See **suitable.**

approve *v.* **certify, endorse, sanction.**
These are all used to signify satisfaction or acceptance. APPROVE, the most general, often means simply to consider right or good (*He approved of her decision*), though it is also used in the sense "to consent to officially" (*The legislature approved the bill*). CERTIFY implies official approval based on compliance with set requirements or standards:

The bank officials certified the check. ENDORSE implies the expression of support, especially by public statement: *The senator endorsed the candidate.* SANCTION usually implies not only approval (*The politician sanctioned the use of public-opinion polls in his campaign*) but also official authorization (*The city council sanctioned the opening of stores on Sundays*).
Antonym: **disapprove.**

approximately ***adv.*** **about, almost, nearly, roughly.**
Core meaning: Near to in quantity or amount (*There were approximately 50 people in the audience*).

apt See **suitable.**

arbiter See **judge.**

arbitrary See **dictatorial.**

arbitrator See **judge.**

archaic See **old.**

arctic See **cold.**

ardor See **passion.**

arduous See **difficult.**

area ***n.*** **belt, district, locality, region, zone.**
All of these nouns name extents of land varying widely in size but having recognizably separate identities. AREA is the least specific as to size and boundaries: *a blighted area in Los Angeles; state parks and recreation areas.* Most often REGION refers to an indefinitely large section with distinctive natural features (*tropical regions of South America*), but the term can denote a more precisely defined geographic unit (*polar regions*). ZONE is usually applied specifically (*the Torrid Zone*); sometimes arbitrarily created boundaries are implied (*a residential zone*). A BELT is distinctive in a single stated respect: *the wheat belt; the Bible Belt.* A DISTRICT is a component, generally rather small and distinguishable by its use (*a red-light district*) or by being a clearly defined administrative unit (*an election district*). A

LOCALITY, also small, is the site of a specific thing or of an event, such as a battle.

argue *v.* **bicker, dispute, haggle, quarrel, squabble, wrangle.** These refer to verbal exchange expressing conflict of positions or opinions. ARGUE can be applied to the action of a debater or an advocate of a cause (*argue in favor of a law*), as well as to that of one engaged in an exchange on the lower level implied by most of these terms (*always arguing with his friends*). The same distinction applies to DISPUTE, but here there is often more suggestion of anger than of reasoning. QUARREL in this sense involves anger and usually hostility as well. WRANGLE stresses noisy display of anger. BICKER and SQUABBLE are applicable to minor quarrels; *squabble* suggests pettiness, and *bicker* implies persistent, bad-tempered exchange. HAGGLE applies to argument engaged in by one seeking the most favorable terms in arranging a bargain (*haggled over the price of the chair*) or in attempting to come to terms (*haggling over the site for peace talks*).

arm See **branch.**

aroma See **flavor.**

arouse See **provoke.**

arraign See **accuse.**

arrest *v.* **1. apprehend, detain.**
ARREST and APPREHEND mean to seize and hold under authority of the law: *arrest a criminal; apprehend a felon.* To DETAIN is to keep in custody: *detain a suspect.*
Antonym: **free.**
2. See **stop.**

artificial *adj.* **ersatz, synthetic.**
These three all refer to what is made by man rather than occurring in nature. ARTIFICIAL is the most neutral term and has widest application (*an artificial sweetener; artificial flowers; artificial pearls; an artificial respirator*); it also describes what is not genuine or natural (*an artificial display of affection*). What is ERSATZ suggests transparently inferior

imitation: *ersatz mink.* SYNTHETIC most often implies the use of a chemical process to produce a substance that will look or function like the original, often with certain advantages: *synthetic rubber; synthetic fabrics.*
Antonym: **natural.**

artsy See **arty.**

arty ***adj.*** **artsy, contrived, precious, pretentious.**
Core meaning: Pretentiously artistic (*an artsy film*).

ascend See **rise.**

ascribe See **attribute.**

assail See **attack.**

assault See **attack.**

assemble See **gather.**

assert ***v.*** **affirm, allege, declare.**
All of these words share the meaning of making a positive statement; they differ in emphasis. ASSERT implies that one states one's position boldly. AFFIRM stresses confidence in the validity of the statement. ALLEGE applies when the statement is apt to raise controversy and is made without proof. DECLARE has about the same force as *assert* but can suggest a formal manner or great authority.
Antonym: **deny.**

assign See **attribute.**

assimilate See **absorb.**

assist See **help.**

associate See **partner.**

association See **union.**

assuage See **pacify.**

assurance 1. See **certainty. 2.** See **confidence.**

astonishing See **fabulous.**

astute See **shrewd.**

atmosphere See **flavor.**

attach *v.* **affix, fasten.**

All of these denote the joining of one thing to another: *attach wires to an electrical plug; affix a label to a package; fasten a button to a skirt. Attach* and *affix* can also refer to adding on: *attach a signature to a document; affix a seal to a will. Fasten* often denotes making fast or secure: *fasten your seat belts.*

Antonym: **detach.**

attack *v.* **assail, assault, bombard.**

ATTACK and its synonyms refer to setting upon, literally or figuratively. *Attack* applies to any violent offensive action, physical or verbal: *The commandos attacked the outpost at dawn. She attacked any speaker whose views differed from hers.* ASSAIL implies repeated and violent attacks: *assailed the fortification; assailed by doubts.* ASSAULT usually—but not always—involves physical contact and sudden violence: *The mugger assaulted his victim in the park. The scientists assaulted the problem.* BOMBARD suggests showering with bombs or shells or, figuratively, with words: *ships bombarding Fort McHenry; bombarding the speaker with questions.*

Antonym: **defend.**

attain See **reach.**

attention See **notice.**

attire See **dress.**

attitude See **posture.**

attract *v.* **captivate, charm, enchant, fascinate.**

ATTRACT and its synonyms all mean to draw by some quality or action. *Attract* is the most general, simply implying the gravitation of objects, substances, or persons: *Light attracts insects. Her vitality attracted his interest.* CAPTIVATE, CHARM, ENCHANT, and FASCINATE all apply to strong, compelling attraction, often of one person to another. *Enchant* suggests an almost magical quality of attraction: *Her green eyes enchanted him. Captivate* and *charm* imply an ability or quality that pleases or delights: *a sense of drama*

that captivates audiences; courtesy that charms even the doubters. Fascinate includes not only the notion of irresistible attraction but also implies the ability to hold another's interest and attention: *The account of his trip to China fascinated his listeners.*
Antonym: **repel.**

attribute *v.* **accredit, ascribe, assign, charge, credit, impute.**
Core meaning: To regard as belonging to or resulting from another (*a painting attributed to Monet*).

atypical 1. See **abnormal. 2.** See **unconventional.**

audacious See **bold.**

augment See **increase.**

augury See **omen.**

auspicious See **favorable.**

austere See **plain.**

austerity See **severity.**

authentic *adj.* **bona fide, genuine, original, real, true, undoubted.**
Core meaning: Not counterfeit or copied (*an authentic Beethoven manuscript*).

authoritative See **dictatorial.**

authority 1. See **power. 2.** See **professional.**

authorization See **permission.**

automatic See **involuntary.**

aversion See **distaste.**

avid See **voracious.**

avoid *v.* **elude, escape, shun.**
AVOID and its synonyms share the sense of getting or staying away from something dangerous or unpleasant. *Avoid* and SHUN are close in meaning, and both imply a deliberate effort to remain out of the range of persons or things considered a source of difficulty: *avoid* (or *shun*) *nosy acquaintances; avoid* (or *shun*) *rich foods.* ELUDE suggests getting

away by cleverness or by a very small margin: *The fly eluded the spider.* ESCAPE often suggests breaking loose from confinement (*escaped from jail*); it can also mean simply to remain unaffected by something harmful or unwanted (*escape injury*).
***Antonym:* face.**

aware *adj.* cognizant, conscious.
These words all mean "being mindful of" and "having knowledge of." One is AWARE of something both through observation (*aware of his hostility*) and by means of information (*aware of the President's veto*). COGNIZANT, a more formal term, stresses having and recognizing sure knowledge: *I am cognizant of the objections of the faculty.* CONSCIOUS emphasizes the recognition of something sensed or felt: *conscious of an undercurrent of fear.*
***Antonym:* unaware.**

awkward *adj.* clumsy, inept, ungainly.
All of these adjectives refer to lack of grace or skill in movement, manner, or performance. AWKWARD and CLUMSY, the most general, are often interchangeable. *Awkward*, however, applies both to physical movement (*an awkward dance*) and to embarrassing situations (*an awkward silence*), while *clumsy* emphasizes lack of dexterity in physical movements: *a clumsy juggler.* INEPT applies to actions and speech showing a lack of skill or competence: *an inept performance; an inept remark.* UNGAINLY suggests a lack of grace in form or movement: *an ungainly teen-ager.*
***Antonym:* graceful.**

awry *adj.* amiss, wrong.
Core meaning: Not in accordance with what is usual or expected (*knew something was awry when she failed to keep the appointment*).

axiom See **law.**

baby See **pamper.**

back *v.* backtrack, fall back, retreat, retrograde, retrogress.
Core meaning: To move in a reverse direction (*kept backing slowly toward the door*).

backtrack See **back.**

backward See **reactionary.**

badge See **sign.**

bald See **bare.**

ban See **forbid.**

barbarous See **cruel.**

bare ***adj.*** **bald, naked, nude.**
These apply to what lacks clothing or any usual or expected covering: *bare feet; a bare hillside; a bald head; mountains bald in the wintertime; a naked boy; naked feet; naked branches; a nude body. Bare, bald,* and sometimes *naked* can be used figuratively to describe what is blunt or without qualification: *the bare announcement that he had left; the bald truth; the naked facts.*
Antonym: **covered.**

barren ***adj.*** **sterile, unfruitful.**
BARREN, STERILE, and UNFRUITFUL describe what lacks the power to produce or support crops, plants, or offspring; figuratively they apply to what is not productive, effective, or rewarding: *barren soil; a barren desert; barren efforts; a desolate, sterile region; sterile pleasures; an unfruitful apple tree; an unfruitful discussion.*
Antonym: **fertile.**

bash See **hit.**

bashful See **shy.**

basic See **radical.**

bear See **carry.**

beautiful ***adj.*** **handsome, lovely, pretty.**
All these adjectives apply to what pleases the senses or the mind. BEAUTIFUL is the most comprehensive and the most widely applicable: *a beautiful day; a beautiful description; a beautiful sound.* LOVELY applies to what inspires ardent emotion rather than intellectual appreciation: *a lovely girl; a lovely thought.* PRETTY often implies a rather limited and superficial kind of beauty: *just another pretty face.* HAND-

SOME stresses visual appeal through regular and harmonious proportions: *a handsome design.*
Antonym: **ugly.**

befuddlement See **daze.**

begin *v.* **commence, initiate, start.**
These verbs all refer to coming or putting into operation, being, motion, etc. BEGIN and COMMENCE are equivalent in meaning, though *commence* is sometimes considered stronger in suggesting initiative: *a plant that is beginning to grow; a play that begins at eight o'clock; commenced composing his new symphony; festivities that commenced with the national anthem.* START is often interchangeable with *begin* and *commence* but can also imply setting out from a specific point (*started for New York early in the morning*), setting in motion (*start an engine*), or bringing about (*start an argument*). INITIATE suggests taking the first steps in a process: *initiated an advertising campaign.*
Antonym: **end.**

belief See **opinion.**

believe *v.* **accept, credit.**
To BELIEVE is simply to take as true or real: *I believe your statement.* ACCEPT implies satisfaction that a statement or explanation is in fact accurate (*I accept your word for it*), while CREDIT stresses trust (*Do not credit gossip*).
Antonym: **disbelieve.**

belittle *v.* **depreciate, derogate, detract (from), discount, disparage, downgrade, minimize.**
Core meaning: To think, represent, or speak of as small or unimportant (*belittled his rival's accomplishments*).

belt 1. See **area. 2.** See **hit.**

bend *v.* **1. bow, crook, curve**
These verbs all refer to changing from straightness to a curved or angular position: *bending his elbow; bend a wire; willows bending in the breeze; a back bowed by age; bowing under a heavy load; crooked his arm around the pack-*

age; a little finger that crooks; a road curving sharply just ahead; curve a metal band.
Antonym: **straighten.**
2. See **dispose.**

benevolent See **kind.**

benumb See **deaden.**

berate See **scold.**

betray See **deceive.**

between See **among.**

bias See **dispose.**

bicker See **argue.**

big ***adj.*** **enormous, gigantic, great, huge, immense, large.**
BIG and its synonyms all apply to what is of considerable size. *Big* is the most general and is often used interchangeably with LARGE. ENORMOUS, GIGANTIC, HUGE, and IMMENSE suggest that which is of extraordinarily large size. GREAT means ''notably big''; in addition it has a number of extended senses that do not apply to physical dimension.
Antonym: **little.**

binary See **double.**

bind See **tie.**

bizarre 1. See **fantastic. 2.** See **strange.**

blame ***v.*** **censure, condemn, criticize, denounce.**
To BLAME is to find fault with: *didn't blame the children for being impatient to open their presents.* CENSURE, CONDEMN, and DENOUNCE all imply the expression of strong disapproval; *censure* is the weakest of the three: *a mayor censured by the press; a treaty that condemned war as a means of solving international problems; denouncing a proposed law.* To CRITICIZE is to judge severely; it often suggests a detailed account of one's objections: *We can criticize the government without fear of punishment.*
Antonym: **praise.**

blank See **empty.**

blast See **explode.**

bloc See **combine.**

block See **hinder.**

blow up See **explode.**

blue See **sad.**

bluff See **gruff.**

blunder See **botch.**

blunt 1. See **dull. 2.** See **gruff. 3.** See **deaden.**

blur See **confuse.**

boast *v.* **brag, crow, vaunt.**
Core meaning: To talk with excessive pride (*boasted about their wealth*).

boiling See **hot.**

bold *adj.* **1. audacious, daring.**
These all refer to what requires or shows courage and resoluteness: *a bold proposal; an audacious plan; a daring idea.* BOLD and DARING, as applied to persons, stress not only readiness to meet danger but also a desire to take initiative: *a bold executive; a daring explorer.* AUDACIOUS intensifies these qualities, often to the point of recklessness: *an audacious test pilot.*
Antonym: **timid.**
2. brash, brazen, forward, impudent, shameless.
All of these describe what shows boldness and effrontery. BOLD implies undue presumption: *a bold glance; a bold reply.* BRASH stresses what is shamelessly bold and even suggests arrogance: *a brash young man who thought he knew everything.* BRAZEN strongly implies open rudeness and insolence: *a brazen remark.* FORWARD applies to one who is unduly self-assertive (*a forward person*) or to what is presumptuous (*forward manners*). IMPUDENT suggests impertinence: *impudent comments made by the children to their grandfather.* SHAMELESS implies lack of a sense of de-

cency, together with contempt for the rights of others: *a shameless liar.*
Antonym: **shy.**

bombard See **attack.**

bona fide See **authentic.**

bond ***v.*** **adhere (to), cleave, cling, adhere, stick.**
Core meaning: To hold fast to (*plastics bonded with cement*).

bondage ***n.*** **servitude, slavery.**
These nouns refer to the condition of being involuntarily under the power of another. BONDAGE emphasizes being bound to another's service with virtually no hope of release: *The Israelites toiled in Egyptian bondage.* The term is also used figuratively: *Cocaine holds an addict in bondage.* SERVITUDE stresses subjection or submission to a master: *involuntary servitude; sees his job as a form of servitude.* SLAVERY implies being owned as a possession and treated as property: *Lincoln abolished slavery in our country.*
Antonym: **freedom.**

bonus ***n.*** **bounty, gratuity, reward, subsidy.**
All of these designate some form of extra payment. BONUS usually applies to money given or paid in addition to what is normally received or strictly due, often in consideration of superior achievement. BOUNTY generally pertains to a sum of money given by a government for performing a specific service, such as capturing an outlaw or killing a destructive animal. A GRATUITY is a voluntary payment, such as a tip, in appreciation of services rendered. REWARD refers broadly to payment for a specific effort or service, as the return of a lost article or the capture of a criminal. A SUBSIDY is a large grant, usually by a government, in support of an enterprise considered to be in the public interest but not self-sustaining.

bony See **thin.**

book *v.* **engage, reserve.**
Core meaning: To claim or secure in advance (*book a function room*).

boost See **raise.**

border *n.* **borderline, brink, edge, fringe, margin, periphery, rim.**
Core meaning: A fairly narrow line or space forming a boundary (*the border of the property*).

borderline See **border.**

bore *v.* **fatigue, tire, weary.**
These apply to what generates tedium because it is uninteresting or monotonous. BORE implies dullness that causes listlessness and lack of interest. FATIGUE, TIRE, and WEARY suggest what makes one lose interest to the point of wanting to go to sleep.
Antonym: **amuse.**

borrow *v.* **adopt.**
To BORROW is to obtain or receive something with the understanding that it—or its equivalent in kind—will be returned: *borrow a book.* It also can mean taking up a word, gesture, attitude, etc., and using it as one's own (*English has many words borrowed from French*); ADOPT is a synonym of *borrow* only in this figurative sense (*adopted her sister's mannerisms*).
Antonym: **lend.**

botch *v.* **blunder, bungle, fumble, mishandle, mismanage, muff.**
Core meaning: To harm severely through inept handling (*a repair botched by an incompetent mechanic*).

bother See **annoy.**

bountiful See **generous.**

bow 1. See **bend. 2.** See **yield.**

brace See **couple.**

brag See **boast.**

branch ***n.*** **appendage, arm, fork, offshoot.**
Core meaning: Something resembling a tree branch (*the eastern branch of the company*).

brash See **bold.**

brave ***adj.*** **courageous, fearless, valiant.**
These are used to describe what has or shows resoluteness. BRAVE implies self-control and resolve in the face of danger: *a brave soldier.* COURAGEOUS and VALIANT emphasize moral strength and standing up for what is right and true: *a courageous social reformer; a valiant struggle against illness.* FEARLESS stresses absence of fear: *a fearless lion.* See also **face.**
Antonym: **cowardly.**

brazen See **bold.**

breach ***n.*** **1. infraction, infringement, transgression, trespass, violation.**
Core meaning: An act or instance of breaking a law or regulation (*a breach in the security system*).
2. break, disaffection, estrangement, fissure, rent, rift, rupture, schism.
Core meaning: An interruption in friendly relations (*tried to repair the breach between the two brothers*).

break 1. See **opportunity. 2.** See **breach.**

breakable See **fragile.**

breakdown See **analysis.**

breed See **type.**

brief See **short.**

bright 1. See **cheerful. 2.** See **clever. 3.** See **intelligent.**

brilliant See **intelligent.**

brink See **border.**

brio See **spirit.**

brittle See **fragile.**

broad ***adj.*** **expansive, extensive, spacious, wide.**

BROAD and WIDE both indicate horizontal extent and are sometimes interchangeable. *Broad* is generally the choice when describing a surface or expanse (*a broad channel*), while *wide* is best for stressing space, such as the distance across a surface, especially when it is measured numerically (*a wide corridor*). EXPANSIVE stresses considerable sweep (*a calm, expansive lake*). EXTENSIVE focuses on the vast area of the space or topic under discussion (*extensive acreage; extensive coverage of the news*). SPACIOUS connotes greatness of size (*a spacious room*).

Antonym: **narrow.**

broadcast See **advertise.**

broker See **go-between.**

brusque See **gruff.**

build up See **advertise.**

bulk ***n.*** **amplitude, magnitude, mass, size, volume.**

Core meaning: Great amount or dimension (*the monstrous bulk of a supertanker*).

bungle See **botch.**

burden See **charge.**

burning See **hot.**

bushwhack See **ambush.**

business ***n.*** **commerce, industry, trade, traffic.**

BUSINESS applies broadly to all gainful activity, though it usually excludes the professions and farming. INDUSTRY is the production and manufacture of goods and commodities, especially on a large scale; COMMERCE and TRADE are the exchange and distribution of commodities. *Commerce* is often applied to exchange of commodities for money, as within a country, while *trade* refers to exchange of commodities for commodities, as between countries. TRAFFIC may suggest illegal trade, as in narcotics. See also **work.**

busy See **active.**

buy *v.* **purchase.**
BUY and PURCHASE, which are basically interchangeable, both mean "to obtain in exchange for money or something of equivalent value." *Purchase,* however, is often considered a more formal term, frequently implying that the transaction may be of some greater importance: *She buys food every Saturday in the supermarket. The entrepreneur purchased the* Queen Mary *as a tourist attraction.*
Antonym: **sell.**

bypass See **skirt.**

cadaverous See **ghastly.**

calamity See **disaster.**

calendar See **program.**

calm *adj.* **peaceful, placid, serene, tranquil.**
CALM and its synonyms describe absence of movement, noise, or disturbing emotion. *Calm* implies freedom from agitation: *a calm acceptance of the inevitable.* PEACEFUL refers to undisturbed serenity: *a peaceful family life.* PLACID suggests that a person is not easily shaken by emotion (*a placid disposition*); as a physical description it applies to surfaces that are unruffled (*a placid lake*). SERENE suggests a lofty, almost spiritual calm (*a serene smile*). TRANQUIL usually implies a calm that endures (*a tranquil lifestyle*). See also **tranquillity.**
Antonym: **upset.**

cancel *v.* **annul, erase, expunge, strike out.**
Core meaning: To remove or invalidate by or as if by wiping clean (*cancel an order*).

cant See **language.**

capable See **able.**

capacity See **ability.**

capital See **excellent.**

capitulate See **yield.**

capricious *adj.* **changeable, erratic, fickle, inconstant, mercurial, temperamental, unpredictable, volatile.**
Core meaning: Following no predictable pattern (*a capricious flirt; a capricious storm*).

captivate See **attract.**

care See **anxiety.**

careful *adj.* **1. cautious, circumspect, prudent.**
These all describe what has or shows caution. CAREFUL is most general: *a careful driver.* CAUTIOUS implies wariness, as if to avoid danger or harm: *a cautious pedestrian.* CIRCUMSPECT and PRUDENT suggest good judgment and discretion: *circumspect in shopping for a used car; a prudent decision.*
Antonym: **careless.**
2. conscientious, meticulous, painstaking.
These all describe what involves or shows effort and close attention. CONSCIENTIOUS also suggests seriousness of purpose and a sense of duty: *a conscientious clerk.* METICULOUS and PAINSTAKING both imply precision and thoroughness: *kept meticulous records; painstaking research.*
Antonym: **careless.**

careless *adj.* **1. heedless, inadvertent.**
All of these refer to actions or attitudes that show a lack of regard for consequences. CARELESS suggests lack of attentiveness: *a careless worker.* HEEDLESS implies inattentiveness to the point of recklessness: *heedless of their warnings.* INADVERTENT applies to unintentional actions: *an inadvertent mistake.*
Antonym: **careful.**
2. shoddy, slipshod, sloppy.
These all describe what is marked by neglect or insufficient attention: *careless typing; shoddy workmanship; slipshod bookkeeping; sloppy writing.*
Antonym: **careful.**

caress *v.* **cuddle, fondle, pet.**
Core meaning: To touch or stroke affectionately (*caressed the little boy*).

careworn See **haggard.**

carry ***v.*** **bear, have, possess.**
Core meaning: To hold on one's person (*I never carry cash*).

cartel See **combine.**

casual See **informal.**

cataclysm See **disaster.**

catalyst See **stimulus.**

catastrophe See **disaster.**

catch ***v.*** **clutch, grab, nab, seize, snatch.**
Core meaning: To get hold of something moving (*couldn't catch the ball*).

caustic See **sarcastic.**

caution See **warning.**

cautious See **careful.**

caveat See **warning.**

cease See **stop.**

censure 1. See **blame. 2.** See **disapprove.**

central See **middle.**

ceremonious See **formal.**

certainty ***n.*** **assurance, conviction.**
These all share the meaning "freedom from doubt." CERTAINTY stresses sureness (*the certainty that the team would win*); ASSURANCE, confidence and even self-confidence (*played tennis with assurance*); and CONVICTION, strong belief (*a conviction that patience would bring the best results*).
Antonym: **uncertainty.**

certify See **approve.**

challenge See **objection.**

chance 1. See **accidental. 2.** See **opportunity.**

change *v.* **alter, convert, modify, transform, vary.** These verbs all mean to make or become different. CHANGE, the most general, involves a basic difference (*change the colors in a picture*) or a substitution of one thing for another (*change clothes*). ALTER usually implies a smaller difference or one only in some given respect (*altered her appearance*). CONVERT can refer to change into another form, condition, etc. (*convert carbon dioxide into sugar*), or to change from one use to another (*convert a cellar into a playroom*). MODIFY often adds to *change* and *alter* the idea of making or becoming less extreme, severe, or strong: *weather that modified in the spring*. TRANSFORM refers to marked change in form, appearance, function, or condition: *A steam engine transforms heat into energy*. VARY implies not only change (*Temperature varies from day to day*) but also divergence (*behavior that varies from the expected*).

changeable See **capricious.**

chaperon See **accompany.**

character See **disposition.**

characteristic *adj.* **distinctive, individual, peculiar, typical.** These indicate a trait, feature, or quality that identifies or sets apart someone or something. CHARACTERISTIC designates the identifying and especially the essential feature: *the zebra's characteristic stripes*. INDIVIDUAL lends to *characteristic* a personal quality that more definitely sets apart the person or thing: *students judged by individual performance*. DISTINCTIVE intensifies the meaning of *individual: Red berries are a distinctive feature of this plant*. PECULIAR emphasizes a trait belonging solely to one person or one thing; in this sense it does not necessarily imply oddness: *a mello sound peculiar to the cello*. TYPICAL, the most common of these terms, describes features, qualities, or behavior broadly applicable to a kind, group, or class: *a typical suburban community*.

charge 1. *n.* **burden, load, tax, weight.** *Core meaning:* A heavy responsibility placed on a person

(*took his charge of the family budget very seriously*).
2. *v.* See **accuse. 3.** *v.* See **attribute.**

charlatan See **imposter.**

charm See **attract.**

chart See **table.**

chaste See **moral.**

chastise See **punish.**

cheap *adj.* **1. inexpensive.**
CHEAP and INEXPENSIVE describe what is low or relatively low in price: *a cheap dress; an inexpensive watch. Cheap* also has a figurative sense meaning "requiring little effort": *a cheap victory.*
Antonym: **expensive.**
2. shoddy.
These describe what is of poor or inferior quality: *cheap, badly made shoes; shoddy toys.*
3. stingy.
CHEAP and STINGY mean "not giving or spending generously": *a cheap escort; a stingy man.*
Antonym: **generous.**

check See **stop.**

cheerful *adj.* **1. cheery, happy, lighthearted.**
All of these describe persons who are in good spirits or behavior that indicates good spirits: *a cheerful waitress; a cheery smile; a happy baby; a lighthearted jest.* See also **glad.**
Antonym: **gloomy.**
2. bright, cheery.
These three describe what produces a feeling of cheer: *a cozy, cheerful room; a bright tune; a cheery fire.*
Antonym: **gloomy.**

cheery See **cheerful.**

cherish 1. See **appreciate. 2.** See **love.**

childish See **immature.**

chilly See **cold.**

choice ***n.*** **alternative, option, preference, selection.**
Each of these involves the privilege of choosing. CHOICE implies broadly the power, right, or possibility of choosing from a set of persons or things: *He left me no choice—he had already bought the green car.* ALTERNATIVE stresses choice between two possibilities or courses of action: *The alternative is between increased taxes and a budget deficit.* OPTION stresses the power or right of choosing: *having no option but to comply.* PREFERENCE indicates choice based on what one finds more desirable: *a preference for chocolate over vanilla.* SELECTION suggests a wide variety of things or persons to choose from: *a selection of books.*

choose ***v.*** **elect, pick, select.**
These all refer to taking one of several persons, things, or courses. CHOOSE implies the use of judgment: *chose a red hat; had to choose between working and studying.* ELECT strongly suggests careful thought in making a selection, usually between alternatives: *elects to go to London instead of Paris.* SELECT stresses care and comparison in choosing from a large variety: *select the right golf club for getting out of the trap.* PICK is the least precise of the group and often implies less deliberation than the others: *pick a pencil.*

chronic ***adj.*** **continuing, lingering, persistent, prolonged, protracted.**
Core meaning: Of long duration (*suffers chronic guilt feelings*).

chubby See **fat.**

circle 1. ***n.*** **clique, club, fraternity, set, society.**
CIRCLE and its synonyms denote a group of associates. *Circle* can describe almost any group having common interests or activities on a scale small or large: *a sewing circle; financial circles.* It can also designate the extent of personal relationships: *her circle of friends.* CLIQUE pertains to a small, exclusive group, usually social, that remains aloof

from others. CLUB can imply exclusiveness but often means only a group devoted to a common interest best pursued in company: *Rotary Club; a bridge club.* FRATERNITY most commonly denotes a social organization of male students; it can also refer to a group of people not actually organized but associated or linked by similar backgrounds, interests, occupations, etc.: *the medical fraternity.* SET suggests a large, loosely bound group defined by condition (*the younger set*), preoccupation with fashionable activity (*the smart set; the jet set*), etc. SOCIETY, in this sense, is usually a formally organized group with common interests, sometimes cultural: *a stamp-collecting society.*
2. *v.* See **surround.**

circuitous See **indirect.**

circumscribe See **limit.**

circumspect See **careful.**

circumspection See **prudence.**

circumvent See **skirt.**

civil See **polite.**

clandestine See **secret.**

clarify *v.* **elucidate, explain.**
These three mean to make clear or easier to understand: *clarify your argument; elucidate the meaning of a phrase; explain the rules of the game; explain the meaning of a poem.*
Antonym: **confuse.**

clash See **discord.**

clean *adj.* **cleanly, immaculate, spotless.**
CLEAN and its synonyms all describe what is free from dirt, stains, or impurities. *Clean* is the most general: *a clean glass; clean water.* CLEANLY means "habitually and carefully neat and clean": *A cat is a cleanly animal.* IMMACULATE and SPOTLESS are synonymous in meaning "perfectly

clean," but *immaculate* is the more formal term: *a spotless* (or *immaculate*) *coat.*
Antonym: **dirty.**

cleanly See **clean.**

clear ***adj.*** **distinct, unmistakable.**
These all apply to what is easily perceived by the eye, ear, or mind. CLEAR is the most general: *a clear picture; a clear voice; a clear statement.* DISTINCT suggests what is well defined: *a distinct outline.* UNMISTAKABLE emphasizes what is readily evident: *an unmistakable resemblance.*
Antonyms: **unclear; vague.**

cleave See **bond.**

clever ***adj.*** **alert, bright, smart.**
These describe persons who are quick to learn, think, understand, etc.: *a clever girl; an alert child; a bright, attractive freshman; a smart lawyer.* They can also be applied to actions, behavior, thoughts, etc., that reveal quick-wittedness: *a clever plan; alert driving; a bright idea; a smart decision.*
Antonym: **dull.**

climax ***n.*** **acme, apex, apogee, crest, culmination, peak, pinnacle, summit, zenith.**
Core meaning: The highest point or state (*a discovery that was the climax of her career*).

climb See **rise.**

cling See **bond.**

clip See **hit.**

clique See **circle.**

cloak See **hide.**

clobber See **hit.**

cloistered See **secluded.**

close 1. See **end.** 2. See **near.** 3. See **stingy.**

clothe See **dress.**

club See **circle.**

clumsy 1. See **awkward. 2.** See **tactless.**

clutch See **catch.**

coalition See **combine.**

coarse ***adj.*** **crude, gross, indelicate, obscene, vulgar.**
As it describes a material property COARSE means "rough in grain or texture." It has a figurative meaning that describes lack of refinement in manners, appearance, or expression (*coarse behavior; coarse language*); its synonyms share this meaning. CRUDE suggests lack of tact or taste: *a crude expression.* GROSS implies crudeness and vulgarity: *a gross remark.* INDELICATE describes what is offensive to propriety: *indelicate comments.* OBSCENE strongly stresses lewdness or indecency: *obscene jokes.* VULGAR emphasizes offensiveness and suggests boorishness and poor breeding: *a vulgar display of wealth.*
Antonym: **refined.**

coast See **slide.**

coax See **urge.**

coddle See **pamper.**

coercion See **force.**

coextensive See **parallel.**

cognizance See **notice.**

cognizant See **aware.**

coincide See **agree.**

cold ***adj.*** **arctic, chilly, cool, frigid, frosty, icy.**
Used literally, these words describe what has a low temperature; figuratively they also refer to lack of enthusiasm, cordiality, personal warmth, etc. COLD is the most general: *cold air; a cold person.* CHILLY and COOL suggest that something is moderately cold (*damp, chilly weather; a cool breeze*) or unenthusiastic (*a chilly reaction to the new plan; a cool reception*); *cool* can also imply that something is calm or unexcited: *a cool head in a crisis.* What is FROSTY is

cold enough for the formation of small ice crystals (*a frosty night*) or very cold and unfriendly in manner (*a frosty reply*). ARCTIC, FRIGID, and ICY all describe what is bitterly cold (*arctic weather; a frigid room; the icy waters of the sea in winter*); *frigid* and *icy* also apply to what is severe or very unfriendly (*frigid dignity; an icy stare*).
Antonym: **hot.**

collateral See **parallel.**

colleague See **partner.**

collect See **gather.**

collusion See **conspiracy.**

combat 1. See **conflict. 2.** See **repel. 3.** See **withstand.**

combine *n.* bloc, cartel, coalition, faction, party.
Core meaning: A group united by a common cause (*a combine of citizens against nuclear arms*).

comic See **laughable.**

comical See **laughable.**

command *v.* 1. direct, instruct, order.
In the sense in which they are compared, these verbs all mean "to demand that a person or group do—or not do—something." COMMAND and ORDER are similar in emphasizing the official authority of the person making the demand: *commanded me to leave; order the staff to be punctual.* DIRECT and INSTRUCT are less imperative; *instruct* in particular suggests a mild order, often a mere direction that a person do something in a particular way: *direct the police to free the prisoners; instructed the soldiers to stand at attention.*
Antonym: **obey.**
2. See **expertise.**

commence See **begin.**

commentary See **review.**

commerce See **business.**

commodities See **goods.**

common ***adj.*** **familiar, ordinary, prevalent.**
These describe what is generally known or often seen, heard, or the like. COMMON applies to what is customary, takes place daily, or is widely used: *a common soldier; when filling stations became common.* FAMILIAR describes what is well known or quickly recognized through frequent occurrence or regular association: *the familiar voice of the announcer; a familiar sight.* ORDINARY refers to what is commonly encountered (*an ordinary day*) or what is average or of no exceptional quality (*ordinary parents whose child was a genius*). What is PREVALENT exists widely or occurs commonly: *Sickness is more prevalent in hot, humid areas than in dry, cool areas.* See also **familiar.**
Antonym: **uncommon.**

commonwealth See **nation.**

communicate See **say.**

companionable See **social.**

compass See **surround.**

compassionate See **kind.**

competent See **able.**

competitor See **opponent.**

complete 1. See **end. 2.** See **full. 3.** See **utter.**

complex ***adj.*** **complicated, intricate, involved.**
These describe things having parts so interconnected that the whole is difficult to understand. COMPLEX and COMPLICATED are similar in indicating a challenge to the mind: *complex ideas; a game with complicated rules. Complex,* however, often implies many varying parts (*a complex system of roads and highways*); *complicated* stresses elaborate relationship of parts rather than number (*yarn snarled into a complicated tangle*). INTRICATE refers to a pattern of intertwining parts that is difficult to follow: *an intricate design.* INVOLVED stresses confusion arising from the mixing together of parts and the difficulty of separating them: *a long, involved sentence.*
Antonym: **simple**

compliant See **submissive.**

complicated See **complex.**

comply See **obey.**

compose See **constitute.**

composure See **equanimity.**

comprehend *v.* **apprehend, grasp, understand.**
These verbs refer to the mental process of perceiving something. COMPREHEND and UNDERSTAND are often interchangeable in the sense of "know." *Understand* in particular specifies knowledge of the significance of a thing distinguished from its mere nature (*He doesn't pretend to understand the universe*); in related senses the word refers to knowledge or insight based on close contact or long experience (*really understands the Indians*) or to sympathy or tolerance (*understands their problems*). APPREHEND suggests mental awareness of something without necessarily implying the in-depth knowledge of understanding: *Do you apprehend my meaning*? GRASP usually implies such knowledge and stresses the process of visualizing or penetrating to the heart of a difficult matter: *grasps the principles of number theory*.

comprise See **constitute.**

compulsory *adj.* **mandatory, obligatory.**
COMPULSORY, MANDATORY, and OBLIGATORY describe what is required by laws, rules, or regulations: *compulsory military service; mandatory attendance; obligatory taxes*.
Antonym: **optional.**

compunction See **qualm.**

conceal See **hide.**

concede See **acknowledge.**

concentration *n.* **confluence, conflux, convergence.**
Core meaning: A converging at a common center (*heavy troop concentrations at the border*).

concern 1. See **anxiety. 2.** See **interest.**

conciliate See **pacify.**

concise *adj.* **laconic, pithy, succinct, terse.**
The idea of stating much in few words is contained in these adjectives. CONCISE implies clarity and compactness through the removal of all unnecessary words: *a concise paragraph.* TERSE adds to *concise* the sense that something is brief and to the point: *a terse reply.* LACONIC often suggests brevity that is almost rude: *a laconic response that merely answered the question.* PITHY implies that something is precisely meaningful and has a telling effect: *a pithy comment.* SUCCINCT strongly emphasizes compactness and the elimination of all elaboration: *a succinct explanation.*

conclude See **end.**

conclusive See **valid.**

concord See **harmony.**

concurrent **1.** See **parallel.** **2.** See **unanimous.**

condemn See **blame.**

conditional *adj.* **provisional, provisory, tentative.**
Core meaning: Depending on or containing a condition (*a conditional agreement*).

conduct See **accompany.**

confederate See **partner.**

confederation See **union.**

conference See **deliberation.**

confess See **acknowledge.**

confidence *n.* **1. assurance, self-confidence.**
CONFIDENCE and its synonyms imply faith in oneself or the state of mind that results from this. *Confidence* suggests faith in one's powers: *Her playing exhibited the confidence that comes from experience.* ASSURANCE even more strongly stresses a feeling of certainty and conviction: *managing a difficult situation with assurance.* SELF-CONFIDENCE denotes

trust in one's own abilities: *At the age of ten children often lack self-confidence.*
Antonym: **diffidence.**
2. reliance, trust.
These all imply a firm belief in the honesty, dependability, or power of someone: *I am placing my confidence in you. She put complete reliance in her friends. You must live up to the trust he has shown in you.* See also **trust.**
Antonym: **doubt.**

conflict *n.* **combat, contest, fight, melee, scuffle.**
These denote struggle between opposing forces. CONFLICT applies to large-scale physical struggle between hostile forces (*armed conflict*), to a struggle within a person (*in conflict about her sister*), and to a clash of opposing ideas, interests, etc. (*a conflict between the evidence and his testimony*). CONTEST can mean either friendly competition (*a skating contest*) or a struggle between rival or hostile forces (*a contest over a senatorial seat*). COMBAT implies armed encounter between two persons or groups (*killed in combat*). FIGHT usually refers to a clash involving two persons or a small group (*a fist fight*) or to a struggle for a cause (*the fight for civil rights*). MELEE and SCUFFLE denote generally impromptu and disorderly physical clashes; *melee* implies confused, hand-to-hand fighting, while *scuffle* suggests hand-to-hand fighting on a small scale. See also **discord.**

confluence See **concentration.**

conflux See **concentration.**

conform See **agree.**

conformist See **conventional.**

confuse *v.* **blur, muddle.**
These verbs share the meaning of making something unclear so that its features or elements cannot be distinguished: *Too many affidavits confused the record. Her distraction blurred her thoughts. The report muddled the issues.*
Antonym: **clarify.**

congress See **union.**

conjecture See **theory.**

connect See **join.**

conquest See **victory.**

conscientious See **careful.**

conscious See **aware.**

consecrate See **devote.**

consent See **permission.**

consequence See **effect.**

consequential See **important.**

conserve See **save.**

consider *v.* **deem, regard.**

These refer to holding opinions or views that reflect evaluation of a person or thing. CONSIDER suggests objective evaluation based on reflection and reasoning: *The committee met to consider her qualifications.* DEEM is more subjective through its emphasis on judgment distinguished from analytical thought: *deemed it advisable to wait.* REGARD may imply personal, subjective judgment: *regard him with skepticism.*

consist (of) See **constitute.**

consolidation See **unification.**

conspiracy *n.* **collusion, intrigue, machination, plot.**

CONSPIRACY and its synonyms denote secret plans or schemes. *Conspiracy* refers to such a plan by a group intent usually on an unlawful purpose: *a conspiracy to overthrow the government.* COLLUSION refers to secret agreement between persons or organizations, usually with intent to deceive or cheat others: *department stores acting in collusion to maintain high prices.* INTRIGUE usually implies selfish, petty actions rather than criminal ends: *office politics and intrigue.* MACHINATION, usually plural, strongly implies crafty, hostile dealing by one or more persons: *machinations that got his supervisor fired.* PLOT stresses sinister means and motives but may be small or large in number of participants and scope: *a plot to kill the emperor.*

constant 1. See **continuous. 2.** See **faithful. 3.** See **true.**

constitute *v.* **compose, comprise, consist (of), form, make, make up.**
Core meaning: To be the constituent parts of (*Ten members constitute a quorum*).

constraint See **force.**

construct See **make.**

consultation See **deliberation.**

consume See **waste.**

consummate See **utter.**

contaminated See **impure.**

contemporary See **modern.**

contest See **conflict.**

continence See **abstinence.**

contingency See **possibility.**

continual See **continuous.**

continuation *n.* **continuity, continuum, duration, endurance.**
Core meaning: Uninterrupted existence or succession (*a continuation of the negotiations*).

continuing See **chronic.**

continuity See **continuation.**

continuous *adj.* **constant, continual.**
These have the common meaning of happening over and over during a long period of time. CONTINUOUS is the most inclusive; it implies either lack of interruption in time or unbroken extent in space: *a continuous supply of oxygen; a continuous line.* CONSTANT in this sense refers only to continuity in time: *Our television has a constant flicker.* CONTINUAL sometimes means "steady" (*a continual rumpus*), but it is more often used to describe regular and frequent

repetition: *the continual banging of the door.*
Antonym: **discontinuous.**

contract ***v.*** **shrink.**
CONTRACT and SHRINK share the meaning of drawing together or growing smaller: *The world seems to have contracted* (or *shrunk*) *with the invention of the communications satellite. Contract* frequently suggests a reversible process; it often implies the existence of a regular pattern of contraction and expansion or contraction and release: *He contracted his biceps. His biceps contracted. Shrink* often refers to an irreversible process: *The sweater shrank in the dryer. Shrink the material before you sew.*
Antonym: **expand.**

contradict See **deny.**

contradiction See **denial.**

contrary ***adj.*** **perverse, stubborn, willful.**
All of these refer to being in opposition to a prevailing order or to prescribed authority. CONTRARY applies especially to a person who is self-willed and given to resisting authority. PERVERSE implies obstinacy and a native disposition to depart from what is considered the right course of action. STUBBORN stresses inflexibility of mind or will and thus strongly implies resistance to authority. WILLFUL often implies unreasoning, headstrong self-determination and refusal to accept authority.

contrived See **arty.**

control See **power.**

contumelious See **abusive.**

convenient ***adj.*** **1. handy.**
These apply to what is suited to one's comfort, needs, or purpose: *a convenient appliance; a handy supply of pencils.*
2. accessible.
CONVENIENT and ACCESSIBLE refer to what is easy to get to: *a convenient shopping center; an accessible airport.*
Antonym: **inaccessible.**

conventional *adj.* **conformist, establishmentarian, orthodox, square** (*Informal*), **straight** (*Informal*), **traditional.**
Core meaning: Conforming to established practice or standards (*conventional dress; conventional social views*).

convergence See **concentration.**

convert See **change.**

convey See **say.**

conviction 1. See **certainty. 2.** See **opinion.**

convincing See **valid.**

convivial See **social.**

cool See **cold.**

core See **heart.**

corpulent See **fat.**

correct *v.* **amend, rectify, redress, reform, remedy, revise.**
All of these refer to making right or improving. CORRECT can apply broadly to any such act (*correct a wrong impression*) but usually refers to eliminating error or defect (*correcting an article before setting it in type*). RECTIFY stresses the idea of bringing something into conformity with a standard of what is right: *rectify a mistake in the records.* REMEDY involves repairing or removing something considered a cause of harm or damage: *legislation to remedy social inequities.* REDRESS usually refers to setting right something considered wrong or unjust: *redress a grievance.* REFORM implies broad change that improves character, as of a person or institution: *reform criminals; reform society.* REVISE suggests change as a result of reconsideration of an earlier course: *revised a paragraph.* AMEND adds to *revise* a more definite implication of improvement through alteration or addition: *amending his will.* See also **true.**

correctness See **veracity.**

correspond See **agree.**

corruption See **vice.**

cosmos See **universe.**

costly See **expensive.**

counsel See **deliberation.**

country See **nation.**

couple *n.* **brace, pair, yoke.**

These denote two of something in association. COUPLE refers to two of the same kind or sort; they are not necessarily—but often are—closely associated: *a couple of oranges; a married couple.* PAIR stresses close association and often reciprocal dependence of things (*a pair of gloves; a pair of pajamas*); sometimes it denotes a single thing with interdependent parts (*a pair of scissors; a pair of eyeglasses*). BRACE refers mainly to certain game birds, as partridges, and YOKE to two joined draft animals, as oxen.

courageous See **brave.**

courteous See **polite.**

covert See **secret.**

cowardly *adj.* **craven.**

These describe what lacks courage. Both COWARDLY and CRAVEN suggest a shameful show of fear, but *craven* implies an especially high degree of cowardice: *a cowardly lion; a craven liar.*

Antonym: **brave.**

coy See **shy.**

crack See **joke.**

craft See **expertise.**

craven See **cowardly.**

craving See **wish.**

create *v.* **establish, generate, produce.**

These verbs share the meaning of bringing into existence. CREATE often implies the production of something by invention and imagination: *create a musical composition.* To ESTABLISH is to set up or found: *established a chain of food stores*. GENERATE is often used metaphorically: *generate ideas*. PRODUCE means both "to manufacture" (*produce parts for machines*) and "to give rise to" (*Poverty often produces despair*).

creation See **universe.**

credit 1. See **believe. 2.** See **attribute.**

crest See **climax.**

critical ***adj.*** **acute, crucial, serious.**
All of these adjectives are applied to conditions or situations to indicate degrees of intensity or significance. CRITICAL implies the arrival at a turning point and the imminence of decisive change, usually accompanied by considerable risk, peril, or suspense: *the critical point in the negotiations; a sick man in critical condition*. ACUTE applies to a somewhat earlier stage, when intensification of unfavorable conditions signals the approach of a crisis: *an acute need for money; acute appendicitis*. CRUCIAL and *critical* may apply to approximately the same point in time, but *crucial* emphasizes change that is likely to shape future events: *a crucial decision*. SERIOUS lacks the implication of great significance and immediate concern that is inherent in the other terms; rather, it suggests what is worthy of concern or anxiety: *a serious wound*.

criticism See **review.**

criticize 1. See **blame. 2.** See **disapprove.**

critique See **review.**

crook See **bend.**

crow See **boast.**

crucial See **critical.**

crude See **coarse.**

cruel ***adj.*** **barbarous, ferocious, inhuman, pitiless, sadistic, vicious.**
These apply to persons, their behavior, their attitudes, etc., when they cause pain, suffering, or hardship to others.

CRUEL implies satisfaction in or indifference to suffering: *a cruel man; a cruel remark.* What is FEROCIOUS is extremely cruel, even savage (*a ferocious attack*), and BARBAROUS adds the suggestion of brutality that befits only primitive or uncivilized men (*Hitler's barbarous acts*). INHUMAN refers to a marked lack of such desirable human qualities as sympathy for one's fellow man: *inhuman treatment.* SADISTIC implies the experiencing of satisfaction from inflicting cruelty on others. VICIOUS suggests native disposition to savage and dangerous behavior: *gave the boy a vicious beating.* PITILESS refers specifically to absence of mercy: *a pitiless massacre.*

cryptic See **ambiguous.**

cuddle See **caress.**

culmination See **climax.**

cultivate See **promote.**

cultivated See **refined.**

cultured See **refined.**

cumbersome See **heavy.**

curiosity See **interest.**

curious ***adj.*** **inquisitive, nosy.**

CURIOUS, INQUISITIVE, and NOSY share the meaning of having or showing a marked wish for information or knowledge. *Curious* most often suggests eagerness to enlarge one's knowledge, but it may also imply an urge to involve oneself unjustifiably in the affairs of others: *a curious scientist; curious about the contents of the letter. Inquisitive,* a more formal word, shares these implications: *an inquisitive mind; inquisitive to know what was in his will. Nosy* always implies excessive and impertinent personal curiosity. See also **strange.**

Antonym: **uninterested.**

current See **modern.**

curse See **afflict.**

curt See **gruff.**

curve See **bend.**

customary See **familiar.**

cut 1. ***n.*** **piece, portion, segment, slice.**
Core meaning: A part severed or taken from a whole (*a cut of beef*).
2. ***v.*** See **lower.**

danger ***n.*** **hazard, peril, risk.**
These nouns refer to exposure to harm or loss. DANGER is the least specific; it can be used to describe any potentially harmful situation: *At night the city is full of dangers.* HAZARD suggests a threat posed by chance or something largely beyond one's control: *the hazards of driving.* PERIL refers to an immediate threat: *His life will be in peril if the oxygen tank fails to work.* RISK stresses chance or uncertainty, but often from the standpoint of one who weighs it against possible gain; therefore it often suggests voluntary exposure to harm or loss: *This venture is a financial risk, but if we win, our troubles will be over forever.*
Antonym: **safety**

daring See **bold.**

dark ***adj.*** **dim, dusky, murky, shadowy, shady.**
DARK and its synonyms indicate the absence of light or clarity. *Dark,* the most widely applicable, can refer to insufficiency of illumination for seeing (*a dark tunnel*), to deepness of shade of a color (*dark blue*), or figuratively to absence of cheer (*a dark view of life*). DIM describes what is faintly lighted (*a dim corner of the hall*); it also suggests lack of clarity (*a dim memory of the accident*). DUSKY applies mainly to the dimness characteristic of twilight (*a dusky room*) or to deepness of shade of a color (*dusky brown*). MURKY usually implies darkness like that produced by smoke, sediment, etc.: *a murky sky; murky water.* SHADOWY implies obstructed light but suggests shifting illumination (*shadowy woods*) and indistinctness (*shadowy*

forms moving underwater). SHADY refers to what is sheltered from light, especially sunlight (*a shady street*), or, figuratively, to what is covertly dishonest (*a shady deal*). ***Antonym:*** **light.**

dash 1. See **spirit. 2.** See **trace.**

day(s) See **age.**

daze ***n.*** **befuddlement, fog, muddle, stupor, trance.**
Core meaning: A stunned or bewildered condition (*fell flat and lay on the ground in a daze*).

dead ***adj.*** **1. deceased, extinct, lifeless.**
DEAD and its synonyms describe what is without life or continuing existence. *Dead* has the widest use; it applies to whatever once had—but no longer has—physical life (*a dead leaf*), function (*a dead doorbell*), currency (*a dead issue*), or usefulness (*a dead language*). DECEASED is a formal term that is used only for dead people. EXTINCT describes both what is burned out (*an extinct volcano*) and what has died out (*The dodo is extinct, and so are the Tudors*). LIFELESS can describe what once had physical life (*a lifeless body*), what does not support life (*a lifeless planet*), and what lacks spirit or brightness (*lifeless colors*).
Antonym: **alive.**
2. See **vanished.**

deaden ***v.*** **benumb, blunt, desensitize, dull, numb.**
Core meaning: To make less sensitive (*a topical anesthetic to deaden the pain*).

deadly See **fatal.**

deathly See **ghastly.**

debacle See **disaster.**

decease See **die.**

deceased See **dead.**

deceitful See **false.**

deceitfulness See **dishonesty.**

deceive *v.* **betray, delude, double-cross, mislead.**
DECEIVE and its synonyms refer to misrepresentation used to victimize persons. *Deceive* itself involves lying or the deliberate concealment of truth in order to lead another into error or to disadvantage. BETRAY implies disloyalty or treachery that brings another into danger or to disadvantage: *betrayed his friend; betraying the confidence of the voters.* To MISLEAD is to cause to gain a wrong impression (*misled by false rumors*); it does not always imply intent to harm. DELUDE refers to deceiving or misleading to the point of rendering a person unable to make sound judgments. DOUBLE-CROSS, a slang term, implies betrayal of a confidence or the willful breaking of a pledge.

decent 1. See **moral. 2.** See **sufficient.**

decide *v.* **determine, resolve, rule, settle.**
These verbs are compared as they refer to making conclusions or judgments. DECIDE, the least specific, overlaps the other terms without conveying their more special meanings. DETERMINE often involves somewhat narrower issues and more detailed solutions: *Determine whether this answer is true or false.* SETTLE stresses finality of decision (*settled the argument once and for all*), and RULE implies that the decision is handed down by someone having recognized authority (*The referee ruled that the play was fair*). RESOLVE implies deliberation and finality of decision or solution: *resolve a conflict; resolve a problem.*
Antonym: **hesitate.**

decision See **will.**

declare See **assert.**

decline See **reject.**

decorum See **manners.**

decrease *v.* **diminish, dwindle, lessen, reduce.**
All of these share the meaning of becoming or causing to become smaller or less, as in size, extent, or quantity. DECREASE is the most general; it implies gradual and steady

decline: *His appetite decreased daily. The pilot decreased the speed of the plane.* LESSEN can be used interchangeably with *decrease* in most contexts (*His appetite lessened daily*) but does not always stress gradualness (*The pain lessened immediately after the drug was administered*). DIMINISH suggests removal and consequent loss: *The king's authority diminished after the revolt. A drought diminished the nation's food supply.* DWINDLE connotes what decreases bit by bit to a vanishing point: *Their savings dwindled away.* REDUCE emphasizes the sense of coming or bringing down to a lower level: *The volume of noise gradually reduced. The workers reduced their wage demands.*
***Antonym:* increase.**

dedicate See **devote.**

deem See **consider.**

deep ***adj.*** **profound.**
DEEP literally describes what lies or extends far below a surface: *a deep pit; a deep wound.* PROFOUND is no longer much used in this literal sense, but *deep* and *profound* share a figurative sense that describes what shows much wisdom and insight (*a deep knowledge; a profound philosophy*) or much feeling (*a deep love; a profound sigh*). See also **intense.**
***Antonym:* shallow.**

defeat ***n.*** **rout.**
DEFEAT and ROUT refer to the fact or condition of being overcome by an adversary or opponent, as in war or in a competition. *Defeat,* the more general term, does not necessarily imply finality of outcome: *Napoleon's defeat at Waterloo changed the course of European history. The Bruins suffered defeat by the Canadiens but won the next game.* A *rout* is an overwhelming defeat, often followed by a disorderly retreat: *the rout of the Persian fleet at Salamis.*
***Antonym:* victory.**

defective See **imperfect.**

defend *v.* **guard, preserve, protect, safeguard.**
These words mean to make or keep safe from danger or attack. DEFEND implies the use of actions taken to repel an attack: *defend the gates of the city; defended his reputation.* GUARD suggests keeping watch: *guarded the house against intruders.* PRESERVE implies measures taken to maintain something in safety: *Ecologists want to preserve our natural resources.* PROTECT suggests providing cover to repel discomfort, injury, or actual attack: *used a rain hat to protect her hair; a medieval city protected by strong walls.* SAFEGUARD stresses protection from danger and often implies action taken in advance: *safeguard valuables by keeping them in the bank.*
Antonym: **attack.**

defensible See **justifiable.**

defer See **yield.**

deference See **honor.**

deficiency *n.* **insufficiency, lack, shortage.**
These all denote the condition of being inadequate in amount or degree. DEFICIENCY and INSUFFICIENCY suggest that minimal requirements for a particular purpose are not being met: *The neglected child was suffering from vitamin deficiency. The bank had a temporary insufficiency of traveler's checks.* LACK can also imply that something is not available: *a lack of electricity.* SHORTAGE in addition suggests something that falls short of a required or expected amount: *a food shortage.*
Antonym: **excess.**

definite See **explicit.**

deft See **graceful.**

defunct See **vanished.**

dejected See **sad.**

delay *v.* **detain, retard, slow.**
These verbs share the meaning of holding back and hindering progress. DELAY applies to putting behind schedule or to

postponing action: *Business often delays his return home. His wife delays dinner then.* DETAIN stresses holding something up at a particular point along the way to completion: *detained by a phone call.* RETARD and SLOW imply a slackening of pace: *snow that retards traffic; winds that slow the car.*
Antonym: **expedite.**

delectable See **delicious.**

delegate See **representative.**

deliberate 1. See **slow. 2.** See **intentional. 3.** See **voluntary.**

deliberation *n.* conference, consultation, counsel, parley.
Core meaning: An exchange of views in an attempt to reach a decision (*the deliberations of the management committee*).

delicate See **fragile.**

delicious *adj.* delectable, luscious, scrumptious.
These all describe what is very pleasing or agreeable to the sense of taste. DELICIOUS, DELECTABLE, and LUSCIOUS can be used interchangeably: *a delicious apple; a delectable piece of cake; a luscious melon.* SCRUMPTIOUS has the same meaning but is informal: *a scrumptious peach.*

delight 1. See **joy. 2.** See **please.**

delimit See **limit.**

deliver See **save.**

delude See **deceive.**

dementia See **insanity.**

demise See **die.**

demolish See **destroy.**

demonstrate See **prove.**

denial *n.* contradiction, disclaimer, negation, rejection.
Core meaning: A refusal to grant the truth of a statement or charge (*issued a denial of the accusations*).

denomination See **name.**

denounce See **blame.**

dense See **dull.**

deny *v.* **contradict, gainsay, refute.**

These verbs have in common the sense of disputing the truthfulness of a statement or a speaker. DENY is the most general and usually implies an open declaration that something is untrue. To CONTRADICT is to assert that the opposite of a given statement is true. GAINSAY is generally used in negative constructions to stress the unlikelihood or impossibility of opposing or rejecting: *raised objections that could not be gainsaid.* REFUTE implies the use of evidence to disprove an opposing claim.

Antonym: **assert.**

depart See **die.**

dependable See **reliable.**

dependent See **subordinate.**

deplete See **waste.**

depravity See **vice.**

deprecate See **disapprove.**

depreciate See **belittle.**

depreciation *n.* **devaluation, markdown, reduction.**

Core meaning: A lowering in price or value (*another depreciation of the U.S. dollar*).

depress See **discourage.**

depressed See **sad.**

deputy See **representative.**

derelict See **abandoned.**

deride See **ridicule.**

derogate See **belittle.**

descend See **fall.**

descendant ***n.*** **posterity, progeny.**
A DESCENDANT is an individual considered as descended from specified ancestors. POSTERITY and PROGENY refer to descendants collectively.
Antonym: **ancestor.**

desensitize See **deaden.**

desert See **abandon.**

deserted See **abandoned.**

designation See **name.**

desire See **wish.**

desist See **stop.**

desolate See **sad.**

desperate See **upset.**

despise ***v.*** **disdain, scorn.**
These verbs all express a feeling that someone or something is inferior and undesirable. DESPISE emphasizes the simple fact of such a negative opinion; the person who despises need not express it to others: *despise unethical behavior.* DISDAIN implies that a feeling of contempt is communicated to others (*disdained her husband's cronies*); SCORN involves the expression of such an opinion, usually with some measure of anger, sarcasm, or ridicule: *scorned his ideas.*
Antonym: **appreciate.**

despotic See **absolute.**

destiny See **fate.**

destitute See **poor.**

destroy ***v.*** **abolish, demolish, raze.**
These all apply to the process of undoing or ruining completely. DESTROY has the broadest application. To ABOLISH is to put an end to: *abolish slavery.* DEMOLISH and RAZE suggest force. *Demolish* implies tearing down: *demolish a house; demolish an argument. Raze* means "to tear down

to the ground; to level'': *razed old tenement buildings.*
Antonym: **create.**

detach *v.* **disengage, unfasten.**
These denote the separation of one thing from another: *detached the gold charm from her bracelet; tried to disengage his leg from the underbrush; unfastened the clasp of a necklace.*
Antonym: **attach.**

detain 1. See **arrest. 2.** See **delay.**

determination See **will.**

determine See **decide.**

detest See **hate.**

detestation See **hate.**

detonate See **explode.**

detract (from) See **belittle.**

detriment 1. See **harm. 2.** See **disadvantage.**

devaluation See **depreciation.**

devious See **underhand.**

devote *v.* **consecrate, dedicate, pledge.**
DEVOTE and its synonyms are compared mainly in the sense of giving oneself or one's effort for a particular end. *Devote,* the most general, implies loyal and close attention to a specific cause, activity, person, etc.: *devoted himself to the care of his mother.* DEDICATE adds the idea of a full and sometimes formal commitment: *a scientist who dedicates himself to research.* CONSECRATE stresses almost sacred commitment to some worthy purpose: *consecrate one's life to improving the lot of the poor.* PLEDGE refers to personal commitment backed by a solemn promise: *The girl's parents pledged their support.*

devotion See **love.**

devout See **holy.**

dextrous See **graceful.**

dialect See **language.**

diatribe See **tirade.**

dictatorial *adj.* **arbitrary, authoritative, dogmatic, imperious, overbearing.**
All of these refer to what has or shows the tendency or disposition to assert authority or to impose control on others. DICTATORIAL suggests the idea of unlimited power and complete authority in the hands of one person; the term stresses a high-handed, absolute manner. ARBITRARY implies that something is based on whim, impulse, selfishness, hasty judgment, or anything other than sound reasoning. DOGMATIC suggests the imposition of one's will or opinion as though it were beyond challenge. IMPERIOUS suggests the manner of one accustomed to commanding. AUTHORITATIVE can apply to what arises from proper authority (*the general's authoritative manner*) or authority based on expert knowledge (*authoritative sources*). OVERBEARING implies a tendency to be domineering and arrogant.

diction See **wording.**

die *v.* **decease, demise, depart, expire, pass away, perish.**
Core meaning: To become dead (*died young*).

differ See **disagree.**

different *adj.* **disparate, divergent, diverse.**
DIFFERENT and its synonyms apply to things that are dissimilar or unlike. *Different* implies distinctness or separateness (*Different people like different things*), sometimes to the point of being unusual (*a really different hair style*). Things that are DISPARATE are entirely dissimilar: *disparate theories about the origin of man*. DIVERGENT suggests that things differ because they extend in different directions: *widely divergent trends*. DIVERSE strongly stresses distinctness in kind (*diverse points of view*); it often describes things that are of several or many kinds (*The United States is a land of diverse people*).
Antonym: **same.**

difficult *adj.* **arduous, hard, troublesome.**
All of these describe what requires great physical or mental effort. HARD and DIFFICULT are often interchangeable (*a hard*—or *difficult—climb; a hard*—or *difficult—task*), but *difficult* is frequently more appropriate when special skill or ingenuity is called for: *a difficult problem.* ARDUOUS suggests burdensome labor or persistent effort: *an arduous journey; arduous training.* TROUBLESOME implies demands that cause worry: *a troublesome child; a troublesome car that stalled often.*
Antonym: **easy.**

diffidence *n.* **shyness, timidity.**
These all denote lack of self-confidence: *diffidence that made it difficult for him to assert himself; shyness that made it painful for him to meet new people; timidity that prevented her from making friends.*
Antonym: **confidence.**

diffident See **shy.**

digest See **absorb.**

dilatory See **slow.**

dilemma See **predicament.**

dilettante See **amateur.**

dim See **dark.**

diminish See **decrease.**

diminutive See **little.**

direct 1. *adj.* **straight, straightforward.**
DIRECT and STRAIGHT share the meaning "not bending or curving": *a direct route; a straight line.* In a figurative sense *direct, straight,* and STRAIGHTFOWARD all describe what is not interrupted or does not deviate or swerve from the point: *a direct descendant; a straight answer; a straightforward explanation.* See also **command.**
Antonym: **indirect.**
2. *v.* See **administer.**

dirty ***adj.*** **filthy, foul, grimy, soiled.**

DIRTY is the most general of these words and describes anything that is physically unclean: *dirty clothes; a dirty floor*. FILTHY and FOUL are more intense and refer to what is extremely and offensively unclean: *a filthy* (or *foul*) *jacket*. *Dirty, filthy,* and *foul* also apply figuratively to what is obscene or indecent: *a dirty joke; a filthy picture; foul language*. GRIMY suggests something whose surface is smudged with soot or other dirt (*grimy hands*); SOILED, something partially stained or dirtied (*soiled laundry*).

Antonym: **clean.**

disadvantage ***n.*** **detriment, drawback, handicap, minus, shortcoming.**

Core meaning: An unfavorable condition, circumstance, or characteristic (*his lack of experience was a major disadvantage*).

disaffect See **estrange.**

disaffection See **breach.**

disagree ***v.*** **differ, dispute, dissent.**

These express incompatibility or lack of agreement. DISAGREE is the most general. DIFFER (*from*) denotes dissimilarity between persons or things that are being compared (*toothpaste differs from toothpowder*); *differ* (*with*), divergence of opinion (*He differed with her on the question*). DISPUTE and DISSENT share the sense of differing in opinion and saying so. *Dispute* implies disagreement expressed in debate or argument. *Dissent* suggests formal opposition to prevailing opinions.

Antonym: **agree.**

disagreeable See **unpleasant.**

disappointment ***n.*** **discontent, disgruntlement, dissatisfaction, letdown, regret.**

Core meaning: Unhappiness caused by the failures of one's hopes or expectations (*not getting the position was a disappointment*).

disapprove *v.* **censure, criticize, deprecate.**
These verbs are used to signify dissatisfaction or rejection. DISAPPROVE, the most general, often means simply to have an unfavorable opinion (*He disapproved of her smoking*), though it is also used in the sense "to refuse to approve" (*The faculty disapproved his request for an extension*). CENSURE implies the expression of strong disapproval: *The press censured the mayor*. To CRITICIZE is both to find fault with (*Newspapers criticized the tax bill*) and to voice criticism (*Jack seldom criticizes or praises*). DEPRECATE also implies the expression of disapproval, often with overtones of regret: *He deprecated the use of force to quell civil disturbances*.
Antonym: **approve.**

disaster *n.* **calamity, cataclysm, catastrophe, debacle, holocaust.**
DISASTER and its synonyms refer to grave occurrences having destructive results. *Disaster* generally implies great destruction, hardship, or loss of life, while CALAMITY emphasizes distress, grief, and suffering more than widespread destruction. A CATASTROPHE is a great and sudden calamity; the term especially stresses the sense of tragic outcome with irreparable loss. CATACLYSM refers to a sudden upheaval that brings an earthshaking change—physical, as an earthquake, or social, as a war. A DEBACLE is a sudden, disastrous collapse, downfall, or defeat. HOLOCAUST implies great or total destruction, especially by fire.

disbelieve *v.* **reject.**
DISBELIEVE, the more general of these terms, can simply imply withholding belief; it may also suggest—as REJECT invariably does—an active, conscious refusal to give credence: *The jury disbelieved* (or *rejected*) *his testimony*.
Antonym: **believe.**

discernible See **perceptible.**

discharge See **fulfill.**

discipline See **punish.**

disclaimer See **denial.**

discontent See **disappointment.**

discontinue See **stop.**

discontinuous *adj.* **intermittent.**
These describe what is marked by breaks or interruptions. DISCONTINUOUS is the more general term; it applies whether there is a single break or many: *a discontinuous line.* INTERMITTENT describes what stops and starts at intervals: *intermittent noises.*
Antonym: **continuous.**

discord *n.* **clash, conflict, dissension.**
These nouns denote a condition marked by disagreement. DISCORD implies sharply opposing positions within a group, preventing united action: *strife and discord within the government.* CLASH suggests sharp conflict involving ideas or interests: *a clash of cultures; a clash between political parties.* CONFLICT in this sense suggests antagonism that results in open hostility or divisiveness: *a personality conflict.* DISSENSION implies difference of opinion causing unrest that disrupts unity within a group: *Dissension prevented the union from accepting the fair settlement.*
Antonym: **harmony.**

discount See **belittle.**

discourage *v.* **1. depress.**
DISCOURAGE and DEPRESS share the meaning of making gloomy or less hopeful: *The sad news depressed everyone. The magnitude of the problem discouraged her.*
Antonym: **encourage.**
2. dissuade.
DISCOURAGE and DISSUADE both imply efforts to prevent someone from doing something: *Friends discouraged him from taking the trip. His invitation dissuaded her from leaving early.*
Antonym: **encourage.**

discourse See **speech.**

discourteous See **impolite.**

discretion See **prudence.**

disdain See **despise.**

disdainful See **proud.**

disengage See **detach.**

disfavor ***n.*** **disgrace, disrepute.**

These denote the condition of being held in low regard. DISFAVOR, the weakest of the terms, suggests mere lack of favor or approval: *His suggestion met with disfavor.* DISGRACE implies strong and general disapproval: *could not stand the disgrace of a divorce.* DISREPUTE involves the absence or loss of reputation: *held in disrepute because of shady business dealings.*

Antonym: **favor.**

disgrace 1. See **disfavor. 2.** See **dishonor.**

disgruntlement See **disappointment.**

disgust See **repel.**

dishonest See **false.**

dishonesty ***n.*** **deceitfulness, duplicity, lying, mendacity, untruthfulness.**

All of these nouns refer to a lack of honesty or integrity. DISHONESTY is the most general. DECEITFULNESS implies a deliberate effort to mislead by falsehood or by concealment of truth. DUPLICITY is both more formal and more emphatic than *deceitfulness;* it often connotes treachery. LYING and MENDACITY, which comes from Latin, both contain blunt accusations of untruth, but *mendacity* suggests a chronic inclination. UNTRUTHFULNESS is a word closely related to *lying* and *mendacity* but softer in tone.

Antonym: **honesty.**

dishonor ***n.*** **disgrace, disrepute, ignominy, infamy, obloquy, odium, opprobrium, shame.**

These nouns refer to the condition of being held in low regard. DISHONOR involves loss of esteem, respect, or repu-

tation: *the dishonor of impeachment.* DISGRACE implies strong and general disapproval: *a coward who lived in disgrace.* DISREPUTE denotes the absence or loss of a good name but is weaker then *dishonor* in suggesting descent from previous high regard: *held in disrepute for his bad conduct.* IGNOMINY often implies public contempt: *the ignominy of failure.* INFAMY is public disgrace or notoriety: *the infamy of the attack on Pearl Harbor.* OBLOQUY implies being subjected to abuse and vilification: *a deposed dictator faced with obloquy.* ODIUM adds to *disgrace* the sense of being widely detested: *the odium of the traffic in drugs.* OPPROBRIUM is the condition of being condemned with scorn: *a term of opprobrium.* SHAME suggests loss of status as a result of a moral offense: *felt shame for the crime he had committed.*
Antonym: **honor.**

disingenuous See **underhand.**

disinterest ***n.*** **apathy, indifference.**
DISINTEREST is merely lack of interest. APATHY is lack of interest in things that are generally found interesting, exciting, or moving: *viewed the great painting with complete apathy.* INDIFFERENCE is lack of any particular interest or marked feeling one way or another: *Whether he took the trip or not was a matter of indifference to him.*
Antonym: **interest.**

disinterested See **apathetic.**

dislike See **distaste.**

disloyal 1. See **faithless. 2.** See **false.**

dismal See **gloomy.**

disorderly ***adj.*** **messy, sloppy, untidy.**
These describe what is not neat or tidy: *a disorderly room; messy old clothes; a sloppy dresser; an untidy appearance.*
Antonym: **neat.**

disparage See **belittle.**

disparate See **different.**

dispatch See **send.**

dispel See **scatter.**

disperse See **scatter.**

display See **show.**

displease *v.* **annoy, offend.**
To DISPLEASE is to cause dissatisfaction, dislike, or disapproval: *an arrogant attitude that displeased his supervisor.* ANNOY suggests bother or irritation: *Your constant complaints annoy your colleagues.* OFFEND applies to what causes anger, resentment, or annoyance: *Her brusqueness offends many people.*
Antonym: **please.**

dispose *v.* **bend, bias, incline, predispose, sway.**
Core meaning: To influence or be influenced in a certain direction (*Her openness disposed me to trust her*).

disposition *n.* **character, nature, personality, temperament.**
These terms all refer to the sum of traits that identify a person. DISPOSITION is approximately equivalent to one's usual mood, attitude, or frame of mind: *an affectionate disposition.* CHARACTER emphasizes moral and ethical characteristics: *a man of bad character.* NATURE suggests those fundamental qualities that determine characteristic behavior or emotional response in people: *It goes against her nature to be dishonest.* PERSONALITY is the sum of distinctive qualities and traits of a person that give him his own individuality: *a man of forceful personality.* TEMPERAMENT applies to the manner in which a person thinks, behaves, and reacts in general: *a nervous temperament.*

disprove *v.* **rebut, refute.**
These all share the sense of establishing that something is false, invalid, or in error by the presentation of opposing evidence or arguments: *disprove a theory; rebut legal arguments; refute a statement.* To *rebut* can also imply weakening the effect of an argument, contention, position, etc.,

without necessarily succeeding: *In a formal debate each side is given an opportunity to rebut the views of the opposition.*
Antonym: **prove.**

dispute 1. See **argue. 2.** See **disagree.**

disregard See **neglect.**

disrepute 1. See **disfavor. 2.** See **dishonor.**

disrespectful *adj.* **irreverent, uncivil.**
Core meaning: Having or showing a lack of respect (*disrespectful of government protocol*).

disrobe See **undress.**

dissatisfaction See **disappointment.**

dissection See **analysis.**

dissemble See **pretend.**

disseminate See **advertise.**

dissension See **discord.**

dissent See **disagree.**

dissipate 1. See **scatter. 2.** See **waste.**

dissolute See **immoral.**

dissuade See **discourage.**

distant See **far.**

distaste *n.* **aversion, dislike.**
These denote feelings of disinclination. DISLIKE is the most general of the three and can often be used interchangeably with the others. The implications of DISTASTE vary, ranging from mild dislike to repugnance. AVERSION suggests strong dislike bordering on repugnance.

distinct See **clear.**

distinctive See **characteristic.**

distraught See **upset.**

distress ***n.*** **agony, hurt, misery, pain.**
Core meaning: A state of suffering (*felt great distress over the death in the family*).

district See **area.**

distrust ***n.*** **doubt, suspicion.**
These denote a lack of trust or belief that something is true, reliable, etc.: *She regarded my proposal with distrust. He is in doubt over the existence of a supreme being. Your excuses inspire suspicion.*
Antonym: **trust.**

divergent See **different.**

diverse See **different.**

diversion See **recreation.**

diversity See **variety.**

divert See **amuse.**

divide See **separate.**

docket See **program.**

dogged See **obstinate.**

dogmatic See **dictatorial.**

dominant ***adj.*** **predominant, preponderant.**
All of these words describe what surpasses all others of its kind in power or importance. DOMINANT applies to what has the most influence or control (*the dominant person in a partnership*) or is unmistakably outstanding (*the dominant building in the skyline.*) PREDOMINANT has the same meanings as *dominant,* but it often suggests superiority that is only temporary (*the predominant city in a changing nation*). PREPONDERANT describes what is greater in weight, number, etc.: *A preponderant number of people voted for the bill, and it passed.*
Antonym: **subordinate.**

dormancy See **abeyance.**

dormant See **inactive.**

dote See **like.**

double *adj.* **binary, dual, duple, duplex, twofold.**
Core meaning: Composed of two parts or things (*a double window*).

double-cross See **deceive.**

doubt *n.* **misgiving, mistrust, suspicion.**
All of these denote a lack of certainty in the honesty, dependability, or power of someone. DOUBT is the most general: *had doubt about Jack's willingness to help.* MISGIVING suggests a feeling of apprehension: *had misgivings about lending him her car.* MISTRUST implies a lack of trust: *mistrust of strangers.* SUSPICION, stronger than *mistrust,* implies the feeling that something is wrong: *eyed the stranger with suspicion.* See also **distrust; uncertainty.**
Antonym: **confidence.**

dour See **gloomy.**

douse See **extinguish.**

downgrade See **belittle.**

draft *n.* **outline, rough, skeleton, sketch.**
Core meaning: A preliminary plan or version (*a draft of the report*).

drain See **waste.**

drawback See **disadvantage.**

dreary See **gloomy.**

dress *v.* **attire, clothe.**
These verbs denote putting clothes on. DRESS is the least specific and most widely applicable: *He dressed the baby. She rarely dressed before breakfast.* CLOTHE often suggests providing clothes as well as putting them on: *It is difficult to feed and clothe such a large family.* ATTIRE suggests fine or formal clothing: *an emperor attired in ceremonial robes.*
Antonym: **undress.**

drill See **teach.**

drive See **ambition.**

drop 1. See **fall. 2.** See **lower.**

drudgery See **work.**

drunk *adj.* **inebriated, intoxicated, tipsy.**
DRUNK and its synonyms apply to people whose coordination and thinking are impaired by too much alcohol. *Drunk,* the most general, and INTOXICATED, a more formal word, mean the same thing; both can also be used to describe immoderate emotion: *drunk with power; intoxicated lovers.* INEBRIATED is rarely used figuratively. TIPSY means "slightly drunk."
Antonym: **sober.**

dual See **double.**

dull 1. *adj.* **dense, dumb, obtuse, slow, stupid.**
All of these describe persons who learn or understand slowly. When they are used in this sense, they are interchangeable, although DUMB is informal in tone and OBTUSE is formal: *brilliant thoughts wasted on a dull audience; a dense, confused pupil; a dumb child; too obtuse to see what the teacher meant; a man who was slow to grasp the drift of the conversation; a stupid boy. Dull, dumb,* and *stupid* can also apply to what is boring, silly, or unintelligent: *a dull book; a dumb play; a stupid solution to the problem.*
Antonym: **clever.**
2. *adj.* **blunt.**
DULL and BLUNT describe objects that are not sharp. *Dull* usually implies that sharpness has been lost through use: *a dull blade. Blunt* more often refers to what is thick-edged by design: *The murder weapon must have been a blunt instrument.*
Antonym: **sharp.**
3. *v.* See **deaden.**

dumb See **dull.**

duple See **double.**

duplex See **double.**

duplicitous See **underhand.**

duplicity See **dishonesty.**

duration See **continuation.**

duress See **force.**

dusky See **dark.**

dwindle See **decrease.**

dynamic See **active.**

early ***adj.*** **premature.**

Both of these words apply to what appears or takes place before its usual or expected time: *a few early robins hopping in the snow; a premature death. Premature* can also suggest undue haste: *a premature judgment.*

Antonym: **late.**

earn ***v.*** **deserve, get, merit, rate, win.**

Core meaning: To receive for one's labor or efforts (*earned a large salary*).

earnings See **wage(s).**

ease ***n.*** **facility.**

EASE and FACILITY share the sense of freedom from difficulty, hard work, or great effort: *play tennis with ease; read music with facility. Facility* emphasizes aptitude: *a facility for learning languages.*

Antonym: **effort.**

ease off See **relent.**

easy ***adj.*** **effortless, facile, light, simple.**

EASY and its synonyms describe what does not require or show much difficulty or expenditure of energy. *Easy* applies both to tasks requiring little exertion (*Dusting the house is easy*) and to persons who are not demanding (*A teacher who always gives high grades is an easy marker*). FACILE and EFFORTLESS stress aptitude and fluency: *a facile speaker; an effortless performance. Facile,* however, sometimes has unfavorable connotations, as of haste, lack of care, lack of sincerity, superficiality, etc.: *a facile solution to the problem.* LIGHT is applied to tasks or chores that involve little

effort: *light housekeeping*. SIMPLE describes what is not complex and hence not intellectually demanding: *a simple game*.
Antonym: **difficult.**

eccentric See **strange.**

eccentricity ***n.*** **idiosyncrasy, quirk.**
ECCENTRICITY, IDIOSYNCRASY, and QUIRK refer to peculiarity of behavior. *Eccentricity* implies deviation from what is normal, customary, or expected; the term may even suggest a disordered mind. An *idiosyncrasy* is more often such a deviation viewed as peculiar to the temperament of an individualistic person and serving as an identifying trait. *Quirk,* a milder term, merely suggests an odd trait or mannerism.

economical ***adj.*** **frugal, provident, prudent, thrifty.**
Core meaning: Careful in the use of material resources (*an economical shopper*).

edge See **border.**

edict See **law.**

educate See **teach.**

effect ***n.*** **consequence, issue, outcome, result, resultant.**
Core meaning: Something brought about by a cause (*high unemployment rates that are effect of the recession*).

effeminate See **female.**

effort ***n.*** **exertion, strain.**
These denote the use of physical or mental energy for the purpose of achieving a desired result. EFFORT has general application: *making an effort to get up; made an effort to move the piano*. EXERTION and STRAIN refer to major efforts, but *strain* often suggests excessive, hence debilitating, use of strength or will power: *Weightlifting involves exertion, but be careful to avoid strain.*
Antonym: **ease.**

effortless See **easy.**

egotistic See **selfish.**

elaborate ***adj.*** **fancy, ornate.**

ELABORATE applies to what is planned or made with great attention to numerous details; it often—but not always—connotes richness and luxury: *an elaborate dinner; an elaborate ball costume.* FANCY in this sense implies intricate and decorative design: *fancy clothes; a fancy bedroom.* ORNATE specifically refers to what is heavily, sometimes excessively, decorated: *ornate carving; an ornate apartment.*
Antonym: **plain.**

élan See **spirit.**

elastic See **flexible.**

elderly See **old.**

elect See **choose.**

elective See **optional.**

elegant ***adj.*** **exquisite, graceful.**

Core meaning: So tastefully beautiful as to draw attention and admiration (*an elegant ball gown; an elegant lady*).

elevated See **high.**

eligibility See **qualification.**

elucidate See **clarify.**

elude See **avoid.**

emancipate See **free.**

embrace See **accept.**

eminent See **famous.**

emolument See **wage(s).**

employment See **work.**

empty ***adj.*** **blank, vacant.**

These three describe what contains nothing, literally and figuratively. EMPTY is the most general in its application: *an empty box; an empty room.* Figuratively it implies a lack of

purpose (*an empty life*), value or meaning (*empty promises*), and the like. BLANK also applies to what contains or is covered by nothing (*a blank wall*); figuratively it describes what lacks ideas or expression (*a blank mind; a blank stare*). VACANT is used to describe what is not occupied or taken: *a vacant mansion; a vacant position*. Figuratively it suggests lack of expression: *a vacant stare*.
***Antonym:* full.**

enchant See **attract.**

encircle See **surround.**

enclose See **surround.**

encourage *v.* **1. hearten.**
ENCOURAGE and HEARTEN share the meaning of lending hope, confidence, or courage: *The doctor's report encouraged the patient's family. Her lawyer's presence heartened the nervous witness.*
***Antonym:* discourage.**
2. urge.
ENCOURAGE and URGE both imply efforts to persuade: *Her husband encouraged her to take the bar examination. The Red Cross urges people to donate blood.*
***Antonym:* discourage.**
3. See **promote.**

end *v.* **close, complete, conclude, finish, terminate.**
These words mean to bring or come to a stopping point or limit. FINISH and COMPLETE suggest reaching the final stage of a task, course, project, etc., and thus often stress accomplishment: *finish a novel; started but never finished; complete a voyage; completed work on his income tax. Complete* can also imply the addition of something missing or needed: *completing an employment application by filling in the blanks*. CLOSE applies to stopping an action, either when it is completed (*The church service closed with a benediction*) or when it cannot be continued (*Lack of support caused the play to close*). CONCLUDE and TERMINATE suggest

formality: *I suggest we terminate this discussion, and I am afraid we conclude on a note of hostility.* END emphasizes finality: *a nice way to end a trip.*
Antonym: **begin.**

endorse See **approve.**

endurance See **continuation.**

enduring See **permanent.**

energetic See **active.**

enfold See **wrap.**

engage See **book.**

enigmatic See **ambiguous.**

enjoy See **like.**

enjoyment See **joy.**

enlarge See **increase.**

enmity ***n.*** **animosity, animus, antagonism, antipathy, hostility.**
Core meaning: Deep-seated hatred (*felt bitter enmity toward the oppressor*).

enormous See **big.**

enough See **sufficient.**

enterprise See **ambition.**

entertain See **amuse.**

entertainment See **recreation.**

enthusiasm See **passion.**

entice See **seduce.**

envelop See **wrap.**

envision See **foresee.**

epoch See **age.**

equal See **same.**

equality See **equivalence.**

equanimity *n.* **composure, nonchalance, serenity.**
EQUANIMITY is the condition or quality of being calm and even-tempered as a characteristic state. COMPOSURE is calmness and steadiness that suggest the exercise of self-control and maintenance of dignity. NONCHALANCE is the real or apparent absence not only of agitation but also of concern, usually shown by an indifferent or casual air. SERENITY is peace and tranquillity of nature that suggest immunity to agitation or turmoil.

equivalence *n.* **equality, par, parity.**
Core meaning: The state of being equivalent (*Einstein asserted the equivalence of mass and energy*).

equivalent See **same.**

equivocal See **ambiguous.**

era See **age.**

eradicate See **abolish.**

erase See **cancel.**

erratic See **capricious.**

erroneous See **false.**

error *n.* **mistake, oversight.**
All three of these terms refer to what is not in accordance with accuracy, truth, right, or propriety. ERROR and MISTAKE may often be used interchangeably: *an error* (or *mistake*) *in subtraction. Mistake* often implies poor judgment: *made the mistake of buying a fur coat when she had to borrow money to pay the rent.* An OVERSIGHT is an unintentional omission or faulty act.

ersatz See **artificial.**

erudition See **knowledge.**

escape See **avoid.**

escort See **accompany.**

esprit See **spirit.**

essence See **heart.**

essential See **necessary.**

establish 1. See **create. 2.** See **prove.**

establishmentarian See **conventional.**

estate See **holding(s).**

esteem See **favor.**

estrange *v.* **alienate, disaffect.**

These verbs refer to the disruption of love, friendship, or loyalty. ESTRANGE and ALIENATE apply when a harmonious relationship has given way to indifference or hostility. *Estrange* is most often used to describe married people and usually implies separation: *Through years of quarreling over money, the couple became estranged. Alienate* is often used in the same way but need not be: *He alienated everyone with his crude behavior.* DISAFFECT usually refers to the disruption or undermining of loyalty or allegiance within the membership of a group: *The revelations about the politician's shady deals disaffected his constituency.*

Antonym: **reconcile.**

estrangement See **breach.**

eternal See **permanent.**

eternalize See **immortalize.**

ethical See **moral.**

ethos See **psychology.**

etiquette See **manners.**

even See **level.**

eventual See **last.**

eventuality See **possibility.**

everyday See **familiar.**

evil See **malevolent.**

exactitude See **veracity.**

examination See **analysis.**

exceed See **surpass.**

excel See **surpass.**

excellent ***adj.*** **capital, fine, first-class, great, prime, splendid, super** (*Slang*), **superb, topflight, topnotch.**
Core meaning: Exceptionally good of its kind (*an excellent picture; did an excellent job*).

excess ***n.*** **superfluity, surplus.**
These all denote the condition of exceeding what is normal or sufficient. EXCESS is the most general in this sense: *overcome by an excess of grief; enough oranges, an excess of apples.* SUPERFLUITY suggests abundance beyond need: *a superfluity of punctuation.* SURPLUS focuses on the amount or quantity beyond what is needed or used: *a surplus of coffee for export.*
Antonym: **deficiency.**

excite See **provoke.**

excusable See **justifiable.**

excuse See **pardon.**

execute See **fulfill.**

executive ***adj.*** **administrative, managerial**
Core meaning: Of, for, or relating to administration (*an executive secretary; an executive committee*).

exertion See **effort.**

exhaust See **waste.**

exhibit See **show.**

exhort See **urge.**

exigency See **need.**

exonerate See **vindicate.**

exotic See **foreign.**

expand 1. ***v.*** **swell.**
These words mean to increase in size, volume, etc. EXPAND, the more general, stresses growth or development

(*expanded her knowledge of French*) or an increase in physical dimensions (*Gases expand when heated*). SWELL often implies expansion beyond normal or usual limits: *The injured ankle swelled.*
Antonym: **contract.**
2. See **spread.**

expansive See **broad.**

expedite ***v.*** **accelerate, hasten, speed.**
These share the meaning of easing and helping progress along. EXPEDITE refers to action that makes for the quick and efficient accomplishment of a given project or purpose: *expedite a loan application.* ACCELERATE, HASTEN, and SPEED all suggest stepped-up activity, growth, progress, or production; *hasten* often adds the suggestion that time is short, while *speed* focuses on actual rapid movement: *measures to accelerate a tax reform; hastened the decision to move; speed delivery of the consignment.*
Antonym: **delay.**

expeditious See **fast.**

expend See **waste.**

expensive ***adj.*** **costly.**
EXPENSIVE and COSTLY describe what is high in price: *an expensive ring; costly jewelry.* They also have a figurative sense meaning "involving great loss or sacrifice": *an expensive* (or *costly*) *victory.*
Antonym: **cheap.**

expert See **professional.**

expertise ***n.*** **ability, command, craft, expertness, mastery, proficiency.**
Core meaning: Natural or acquired facility in a specific activity (*tremendous managerial expertise*).

expertness See **expertise.**

expire See **die.**

explain See **clarify.**

explanation *n.* **account, justification, rationale, rationalization, reason.**
Core meaning: A statement of causes or motive (*an explanation of the purpose of the project*).

explicit *adj.* **definite, specific.**
What is EXPLICIT is expressed with precision and in such a way that misunderstanding is difficult or impossible: *gave explicit instructions about selling her property*. DEFINITE refers to what is clearly defined and exact: *a definite plan; a definite time*. SPECIFIC describes what is precisely set forth and complete with any necessary details: *specific questions; specific qualifications*.
Antonym: **implicit.**

explode *v.* **blast, blow up, burst, detonate.**
Core meaning: To release energy violently and suddenly, especially with a loud noise (*a bomb that exploded in midair*).

expose See **show.**

express See **say.**

expunge See **cancel.**

exquisite See **elegant.**

extemporize See **improvise.**

extend See **spread.**

extended See **long.**

extensive See **broad.**

exterminate See **abolish.**

extinct See **dead.**

extinguish *v.* **douse, quench.**
These are compared as they refer to putting out a fire or light: *the wind extinguishing the candles; doused the campfire; dousing the lights in the living room; quenched the lamp*. See also **abolish.**
Antonym: **ignite.**

extirpate See **abolish.**

extraordinary See **uncommon.**

extreme See **intense.**

fabricate See **make.**

fabulous *adj.* **amazing, astonishing, incredible, marvelous, miraculous, phenomenal, stupendous, unbelievable, wonderful, wondrous.**
Core meaning: So remarkable as to cause disbelief (*the fabulous endurance of a long-distance runner*).

face *v.* **brave, meet.**
These share the meaning of confronting or dealing with something boldly or courageously. FACE and MEET are the most neutral: *She has faced danger many times. He meets adversity with fortitude.* BRAVE more strongly stresses self-control and resolve in the face of danger: *soldiers braving a bombardment by the enemy.*
Antonym: **avoid.**

facile 1. See **easy. 2.** See **glib.**

facility See **ease.**

faction See **combine.**

fail *v.* **miscarry.**
These two denote lack of success in a chosen activity or enterprise. FAIL applies generally: *He succeeded where all others had failed. The League of Nations failed to establish world peace.* MISCARRY means to go wrong or to be unsuccessful; it is a somewhat more formal word: *Our plans have all miscarried.*
Antonym: **succeed.**

failing See **weakness.**

fair *adj.* **impartial, just.**
FAIR and its synonyms describe persons, thoughts, and deeds that show proper and equal consideration for all parties and factors concerned in a matter. *Fair* has the widest

application. IMPARTIAL suggests lack of prejudice and freedom from favoritism or preconceived opinion: *an impartial judge*. JUST implies honesty and impartiality (*a just decision*) and conformity to legal and ethical principles (*a just punishment*).
Antonym: **unfair.**

fairly ***adv.*** **impartially, justly.**
Core meaning: In a just way (*settled the dispute fairly*).

faith See **trust.**

faithful ***adj.*** **constant, loyal, staunch, steadfast.**
These refer to what is firm and unchanging in attachment to a person, cause, or the like. FAITHFUL, CONSTANT, and LOYAL stress long and undeviating attachment: *faithful service; a constant friend; loyal followers*. STEADFAST and especially STAUNCH suggest both strong attachment and willingness to lend support when it is needed: *steadfast believers; a staunch ally*. See also **true.**
Antonym: **faithless.**

faithless ***adj.*** **disloyal, false, treacherous.**
These refer to what is unworthy of trust or in violation of it. FAITHLESS implies failure to honor obligations or to fulfill promises: *a faithless husband*. DISLOYAL applies to those who do not give allegiance where it is due: *a traitor, disloyal to king and country*. FALSE refers to persons who are neither loyal nor dutiful: *a false friend*. TREACHEROUS applies to persons who knowingly betray a confidence or trust: *a treacherous ally*.
Antonym: **faithful.**

fake See **improvise.**

faker See **impostor.**

fall ***v.*** **descend, drop.**
These verbs denote a moving downward; FALL and DROP in particular have many extended senses. *Fall* often applies to descent caused by the pull of gravity: *The bombs fell, and the flames sparkled. Drop* implies falling or letting fall from

a higher to a lower place or position: *A penny dropped from his pocket. She dropped a dish on the floor. Fall* and *drop* are also used figuratively to indicate a decrease, as in value or intensity: *Prices on the stock exchange are falling* (or *dropping*). *Her fever dropped* (or *fell*). To DESCEND is simply to come or go down (*an airplane descending for the landing; descended the stairs*); it can also mean to arrive in an overwhelming manner (*relatives who descended on us for the weekend*), to come down from an origin (*an emperor descended from the gods*), and to pass by inheritance (*His estate descended to his daughters*).
Antonym: **rise.**

fallacious ***adj.*** **illogical, invalid, sophistic, specious, spurious.**
Core meaning: Containing errors in reasoning (*fallacious logic*).

fall back See **back.**

false ***adj.*** **1. erroneous, inaccurate, incorrect, wrong.**
These describe what is in error or contrary to fact or truth: *a false statement; a false answer; an erroneous conclusion; an inaccurate description; incorrect figures; a wrong answer.*
Antonym: **true.**
2. dishonest, untruthful.
These words describe what shows or results from falseness or fraud: *a false accusation; a dishonest answer; untruthful testimony.*
Antonym: **true.**
3. deceitful.
These two describe what is calculated to mislead: *false promises; deceitful advertising.*
Antonym: **true.**
4. disloyal, treacherous, unfaithful.
These terms apply to persons who lack loyalty or betray a trust: *a false friend; a disloyal servant; a treacherous lawyer; an unfaithful wife.* See also **faithless.**
Antonym: **true.**

falsehood See **lie.**

falsity See **lie.**

falter See **hesitate.**

famed See **famous.**

familiar *adj.* **common, customary, everyday, frequent, ordinary, usual.**
FAMILIAR and its synonyms describe what is well known and encountered often: *a familiar sight; a familiar excuse; a common weed; the customary fee; an everyday occurrence; a frequent visitor; a dress of an ordinary size; the usual traffic jam during rush hour.* See also **common.**
Antonym: **strange.**

famous *adj.* **eminent, famed, renowned.**
These words describe what has attracted widespread and often favorable notice. FAMOUS and FAMED are the most neutral: *a famous soprano; a famous book; a famed author; a famed ocean liner.* EMINENT describes what is distinguished or outstanding in some respect (*an eminent scientist*); RENOWNED, what is widely honored and acclaimed (*a renowned orator; a renowned university*).
Antonym: **obscure.**

fancy **1.** See **elaborate. 2.** See **imagination. 3.** See **like.**

fantastic *adj.* **bizarre, grotesque.**
FANTASTIC and its synonyms apply to what is very strange or strikingly unusual. *Fantastic* often describes what seems to have slight relation to the real world because of its strangeness or extravagance: *all sorts of fantastic figures and designs.* BIZARRE stresses oddness of character or appearance that shocks or fascinates: *a bizarre hat.* GROTESQUE refers mainly to what is ludicrously distorted or odd in appearance or aspect: *a grotesque monster.*

fantasy See **imagination.**

far *adj.* **distant, remote.**
All of these refer to what is widely removed in space or, less often, in time. DISTANT can be used with a figure to indicate

a specific separation (*20 miles distant*), or it can indicate an indefinite but sizable separation (*the distant past; distant lands*). FAR implies a wide but indefinite distance: *a far country*. REMOTE suggests isolation as well as distance: *a remote Arctic island*.
***Antonym:* near.**

fascinate See **attract.**

fashion 1. *n.* style, vogue.
All of these nouns refer to the prevailing or preferred practice in dress, manners, behavior, etc., at a given time. FASHION, the broadest term, applies to custom or practice that follows the conventions determined by those viewed as leaders: *the latest fashion*. STYLE is sometimes used interchangeably with *fashion* (*the latest style*), but *style* can also suggest what is elegant, distinguished, etc. (*living in style*). VOGUE is applied to what is fashionable or stylish at a given time (*Tiffany glass was in vogue in the early 1900's*); frequently the term suggests enthusiastic acceptance of something for a rather short period (*novels that enjoyed a vogue in the 1930's*). See also **method.**
2. *v.* See **make.**

fast *adj.* expeditious, hasty, quick, rapid, speedy, swift.
FAST, QUICK, RAPID, SPEEDY, and SWIFT describe what acts, moves, happens, or is accomplished in a brief space of time: *a fast runner; a fast train; a quick trip; rapid progress; a speedy reply; a swift response*. EXPEDITIOUS combines the senses of speed and efficiency: *The most expeditious transportation will be used for mail deliveries*. HASTY suggests hurried action and often lack of care and thought: *a hasty judgment*.
***Antonym:* slow.**

fasten See **attach.**

fat *adj.* chubby, corpulent, obese, plump, stout.
These mean having an abundance of flesh, often to excess. FAT, CORPULENT, and OBESE always imply excessive bodily fat: *our fat friend; a corpulent executive; an obese patient*.

CHUBBY and PLUMP suggest pleasing roundness: *a chubby face; a plump figure.* STOUT describes a thickset, bulky figure: *a stout, stern-faced matron.*
Antonym: **thin.**

fatal ***adj.*** **deadly, lethal, mortal.**
FATAL describes conditions, circumstances, or events that have produced death or are destined inevitably to cause death or dire consequences: *a fatal illness; a fatal blow.* DEADLY applies to persons or things capable of killing or, in figurative usage, of producing severe hardship: *a deadly weapon; deadly strain.* MORTAL can describe a person likely to cause death (*a mortal enemy*) or a condition or action that has in fact produced death (*a mortal wound*). LETHAL refers to something that acts or can act as a sure agent of death: *a lethal dose of a drug; a lethal weapon.*

fate ***n.*** **destiny, kismet, lot, predestination.**
Core meaning: That which is inevitably destined (*Her fate was to lead a nation*).

fatigue See **bore.**

faultless See **perfect.**

faulty See **imperfect.**

favor ***n.*** **esteem, regard.**
These nouns denote the condition of holding or being held in good repute. FAVOR implies approval or support: *Her paper was received with favor. The idea of a national health plan is gaining favor with many legislators.* ESTEEM in addition suggests respect: *His accomplishments won him universal esteem.* REGARD adds the connotation of affection: *showed regard for her parents.*
Antonym: **disfavor.**

favorable ***adj.*** **auspicious, propitious.**
These three describe what is beneficial or points to a successful outcome. FAVORABLE has the widest application: *favorable winds; a favorable book review; a favorable impression; favorable signs of recovery.* AUSPICIOUS applies to what shows signs of a successful result: *an auspicious be-*

ginning for the business venture. PROPITIOUS suggests time, place, or circumstance considered as contributors to success: *a propitious spot for peace talks; a climate propitious to the growth of orchids.*
Antonym: **unfavorable.**

fearless See **brave.**

feasible See **possible.**

federation See **union.**

fee See **wage(s).**

feeling ***n.*** **1. idea, impression, intuition, suspicion.**
Core meaning: Intuitive cognition (*I have a feeling we'll get the contract*).
2. See **opinion.**

feign See **pretend.**

fellowship See **union.**

female ***adj.*** **effeminate, feminine, ladylike, womanly.**
FEMALE and FEMININE are essentially classifying terms. *Female* merely categorizes by sex; it is also applicable to animals, plants, and even things: *the female population; a female rabbit; a female socket. Feminine* can be used to categorize (*the feminine lead in a drama*), but it can also describe traits, good and bad, considered characteristic of women (*feminine allure; feminine wiles*). EFFEMINATE is almost always restricted in reference to men and things; it indicates lack of manliness or strength: *an effeminate walk.* LADYLIKE applies to what befits women of good breeding: *ladylike behavior.* WOMANLY describes things that become a woman: *womanly grace.*
Antonym: **male.**

feminine See **female.**

ferocious See **cruel.**

fertile ***adj.*** **fruitful, prolific.**
These all describe what has the power to produce or support crops, plants, and offspring; figuratively they apply to

what suggests growth and abundance, as of ideas, thoughts, and works. FERTILE is the most general term: *a fertile field; a fertile imagination.* FRUITFUL stresses what is conducive to productivity and beneficial results: *a fruitful rain; a fruitful discussion.* PROLIFIC emphasizes large and rapid output (*Rabbits are prolific animals*); used figuratively it is sometimes disparaging (*a prolific writer who turned out a novel a month*).
Antonym: **barren.**

fervor See **passion.**

festivity See **gaiety.**

feverish See **hot.**

fickle See **capricious.**

fiction See **lie.**

fiddle ***v.*** **fidget, fool, monkey, play, tinker, toy, trifle.**
Core meaning: To move one's fingers or hands in a nervous or aimless fashion (*fiddled with the papers on her desk*).

fidelity See **veracity.**

fidget See **fiddle.**

fiery See **hot.**

fight 1. See **conflict. 2.** See **repel. 3.** See **withstand.**

figure See **add.**

filthy See **dirty.**

final See **last.**

find ***v.*** **recover.**
As a synonym of *find,* RECOVER denotes getting back or regaining. *The police recovered the stolen car.* FIND shares this meaning (*Did you ever find your keys?*), but it is also used to mean coming upon something by chance or accident (*found the keys on the table*) and looking for and discovering (*Help me find my wallet*).
Antonym: **lose.**

fine See **excellent.**

finish See **end.**

firm See **hard.**

first ***adj.*** **foremost, inaugural, initial.**

FIRST and its synonyms refer to what marks a beginning. *First* itself applies to what comes before all others, as in a series, sequence, or any collection of like things: *the first month of the year; the first chapter in the book.* FOREMOST refers to what is first in rank or position and therefore leading: *the world's foremost authority on marine biology.* INAUGURAL is applied to what marks a formal beginning or introduction: *an inaugural flight.* INITIAL describes what occurs at the very beginning: *The initial reaction to the plan was unenthusiastic.*

Antonym: **last.**

first-class See **excellent.**

fissure See **breach.**

fit See **suitable.**

fitness See **qualification.**

fitting See **suitable.**

flagrant ***adj.*** **glaring, gross, rank.**

These refer to what is outstandingly bad, evil, erroneous, etc. FLAGRANT and GLARING both stress that what gives cause for concern or offense is unmistakable and conspicuous. *Glaring* is somewhat more emphatic in suggesting what cannot escape notice (*a glaring error*), but *flagrant* often implies that something is deliberately shocking (*a flagrant violation of the rules*). GROSS emphasizes that an offense or failing is so extreme that it cannot be overlooked or condoned: *a gross miscarriage of justice.* RANK, like *flagrant,* sometimes implies an affront to decency; it is often used as an intensifying term with the force of "complete" or "utter": *a rank amateur.* See also **outrageous.**

flash See **moment.**

flat 1. See **level. 2.** See **stale.**

flavor ***n.*** **aroma, atmosphere, savor.**
Core meaning: A distinctive yet intangible quality deemed typical of a given thing (*a city imbued with the flavor of the Orient*).

flawless See **perfect.**

fleeting See **temporary.**

flexible ***adj.*** **elastic, pliant, supple.**
FLEXIBLE and its synonyms describe what literally can be bent or what figuratively can undergo change or modification. *Flexible* and PLIANT are closely related in meaning: *flexible wire; a flexible administrator; flexible plans; pliant material; a pliant personality*. What is ELASTIC returns to its original or normal shape or arrangement after being stretched, compressed, etc. (*an elastic band*), can adapt or be adapted to differing circumstances (*an elastic clause in the contract*), and is quick to recover or revive, as from illness, misfortune, etc. (*an elastic spirit*). SUPPLE describes what is easily bent (*supple leather*), is agile or limber (*a supple body*), or is adaptable (*a supple mind*).
Antonym: **inflexible.**

flimsy See **implausible.**

flip See **glib.**

flourish See **succeed.**

flush See **level.**

fog See **daze.**

foible See **weakness.**

follow See **obey.**

fondle See **caress.**

fondness See **love.**

fool See **fiddle.**

foolish ***adj.*** **preposterous, silly.**
These three describe persons, ideas, deeds, etc., that have or show a lack of good sense or judgment. FOOLISH implies

poor judgment and lack of wisdom: *a foolish young fellow; a foolish investment of time and energy*. SILLY suggests that which shows lack of intelligence, purpose, meaning, etc.: *silly mistakes; a silly question; a silly child who constantly laughed for no reason*. PREPOSTEROUS describes what is completely unreasonable, to the point of being nonsensical: *the preposterous idea of wearing a bikini during a snowstorm*.

forbear See **refrain.**

forbearing See **patient.**

forbid *v.* **ban, prohibit.**
These three verbs all imply a refusal to allow something to be done or an order that prevents someone from doing something. FORBID, the least formal, is also most often used when personal relationships are involved; it suggests that compliance is expected: *The law forbids robbery. I forbid you to go*. PROHIBIT and BAN imply prevention by law or authority: *laws to prohibit discrimination; finally banning billboards on highways*.
Antonym: **permit.**

force *n.* **coercion, constraint, duress, pressure, strength, violence.**
Core meaning: Power used to overcome resistance (*used force to obtain a confession*).

forebear See **ancestor.**

forefather See **ancestor.**

foreign *adj.* **alien, exotic.**
All these describe what is of or from another country or part of the world: *a foreign language; alien workers; exotic birds*. *Alien* often carries connotations of unfamiliarity or strangeness (*an alien custom*), and *exotic* of the charm of the unfamiliar (*an exotic beauty*).
Antonym: **native.**

foreknow See **foresee.**

foremost See **first.**

foresee *v.* **anticipate, envision, foreknow, see.**
Core meaning: To know in advance (*difficulties no one could foresee*).

forewarning See **warning.**

forget *v.* **repress.**
To FORGET is to be unable or to fail to remember: *She forgets telephone numbers. He forgot where he put his cuff links.* Unlike *forget,* REPRESS implies a forcible effort to drive memories, fears, or thoughts from the conscious mind: *She repressed the details of the murder she had witnessed.*
Antonym: **remember.**

forgive See **pardon.**

fork See **branch.**

forlorn See **abandoned.**

form See **constitute.**

formal *adj.* **ceremonious.**
FORMAL and CEREMONIOUS describe what is in accordance with accepted forms, conventions, or rules. *Ceremonious* implies adherence to a set of prescribed rites: *a ceremonious midnight mass. Formal* is the less specific and more widely applicable term: *a formal discussion; a formal wedding announcement.*
Antonym: **informal.**

forsake See **abandon.**

forsaken See **abandoned.**

fortuitous See **accidental.**

fortunate *adj.* **happy, lucky.**
FORTUNATE and the less formal LUCKY can be used interchangeably to refer to what meets with or brings unexpected good fortune, success, etc.: *a fortunate* (or *lucky*) *girl; a fortunate* (or *lucky*) *choice.* HAPPY, which in this sense stresses that something is favorable, is rarely used to describe persons: *a happy circumstance; a happy outcome.*
Antonym: **unfortunate.**

forward See **bold.**

foster See **promote.**

foul See **dirty.**

fragile ***adj.*** **breakable, brittle, delicate, frangible.**
Core meaning: Easily broken or damaged (*a fragile crystal glass; a fragile economy*).

frailty See **weakness.**

frangible See **fragile.**

frantic See **upset.**

fraternity See **circle.**

free ***v.*** **emancipate, liberate, release.**
FREE and its synonyms share the sense of setting at liberty, as from confinement, oppression, the control of others, etc. *Free,* LIBERATE, and RELEASE are the most general and are often interchangeable: *free an innocent man; liberate slaves; releasing prisoners from an internment camp.* EMANCIPATE usually applies more narrowly to setting free from bondage or restraint: *emancipate serfs.*

freedom ***n.*** **liberty, license.**
These refer to the power to speak, think, and act without restraint. FREEDOM and LIBERTY are sometimes used interchangeably, but *freedom* is the more general term: *gave slaves their freedom; had the freedom to contradict the boss. Liberty* often denotes the political condition in which individual rights are defined and guaranteed by law: *The Magna Carta is known as the cornerstone of English liberty.* LICENSE implies the freedom to deviate from prevailing rules or standards: *poetic license.*

frequent See **familiar.**

fresh ***adj.*** **new, novel.**
FRESH, NEW, and NOVEL describe what has very recently been made, put into service, gathered, or the like. *Fresh* and *new* apply widely and generally: *fresh bread; fresh sheets; fresh vegetables; a new nation; new blankets; new corn.* Both words also describe what is recent, original, and

different: *a fresh approach to old problems; new techniques of typesetting. Novel* stresses striking originality: *a novel treatment of folk songs.* See also **new.**
Antonym: **stale.**

freshness See **novelty.**

friendly ***adj.*** **amicable.**
FRIENDLY describes what is marked by or shows friendship: *friendly cooperation; a friendly letter; a friendly gathering; a friendly official.* AMICABLE is a somewhat more formal term: *had an amicable discussion; parted on amicable terms.*
Antonym: **unfriendly.**

frighten ***v.*** **alarm, scare, startle, terrify.**
These verbs share the meaning of causing to feel or feeling fear. FRIGHTEN and SCARE are the most general terms; while *scare* is less formal, the two are often interchangeable: *The crash frightened us. Some children frighten easily. Loud noises scare me.* ALARM implies the sudden onset of fear or apprehension caused by the realization of danger: *Mrs. Danvers was alarmed when Betty's fever suddenly shot up to 104°.* STARTLE suggests sudden surprise or shock: *The doorbell startled me.* TERRIFY implies overwhelming, even paralyzing fear: *The sight of blood terrifies her.*

frightful See **unspeakable.**

frigid See **cold.**

fringe See **border.**

fritter See **waste.**

frosty See **cold.**

frugal See **economical.**

fruitful See **fertile.**

fulfill ***v.*** **discharge, execute, implement, perform.**
Core meaning: To carry out the functions or requirements of (*fulfilled my side of the bargain*).

full ***adj.*** **complete, replete.**

FULL describes what holds all that is normal or possible: *a full pail.* Together with COMPLETE it applies to what has everything necessary, usual, normal, wanted, etc.: *full* (or *complete employment; a complete* (or *full*) *meal. Full* (*of*) and REPLETE (*with*) describe what has a great number or quantity of something, but *replete* stresses plenty and abundance: *shelves full of books; an examination full of errors; a land replete with* (or *full of*) *streams and forests.*

Antonym: **empty.**

fulsome See **unctuous.**

fumble See **botch.**

fun See **gaiety.**

function See **operate.**

functional See **practical.**

fundamental See **radical.**

funny See **laughable.**

further See **advance.**

furtive See **secret.**

fury See **anger.**

gag See **joke.**

gaiety ***n.*** **1. glee, hilarity, jollity, merriment, mirth.**

Core meaning: A state of joyful exuberance (*a house that rang with Christmas gaiety*).

2. festivity, fun, merrymaking, revelry.

Core meaning: Joyful, exuberant activity (*invited the guests to join the gaiety*).

gain See **reach.**

gainsay See **deny.**

gape See **gaze.**

gather ***v.*** **accumulate, amass, assemble, collect.**

These five verbs denote bringing or coming together in a group or mass. GATHER is the most general term: *gather*

flowers; gather information; a crowd gathering for a picnic. COLLECT is often interchangeable with *gather* (*collect*—or *gather*—*firewood; a crowd collecting*—or *gathering*—*for a picnic*), but it is also used to imply careful selection of related things that become part of an organized whole (*collect antiques; collect art*). ACCUMULATE and AMASS refer to the gradual increase of something over a period of time: *amass a fortune; amass knowledge; snow accumulating on the sidewalk; accumulated data.* ASSEMBLE suggests convening out of common interest or purpose: *classes that assembled in the auditorium.*
Antonym: **scatter.**

gaunt See **thin.**

gaze *v.* **gape, glare, ogle, peer, stare.**
All of these verbs refer to looking long and fixedly. To GAZE is usually to look intently and for a long time, as in wonder, fascination, awe, or admiration: *The tourists gazed at the wild beauty of the countryside.* GAPE suggests a prolonged, open-mouthed look reflecting amazement, stupidity, etc.: *gaping at the acrobats.* To GLARE is to fix another with a hard, hostile look: *glared at me with resentment.* To OGLE is to stare impertinently, often in a way that indicates improper interest: *ogling young girls on the street.* To PEER is to look narrowly and searchingly and seemingly with difficulty: *I peered at the small type of the telephone book.* STARE stresses steadiness of gaze and often indicates marked curiosity, boldness, surprise, etc.: *Bill stared at the candy.*

general See **public.**

generate See **create.**

generous *adj.* **bountiful, liberal.**
These adjectives describe what has or shows willingness to give or share. GENEROUS and LIBERAL are often interchangeable: *a generous* (or *liberal*) *contributor to worthy causes; a generous* (or *liberal*) *gift. Generous, liberal,* and BOUNTIFUL can all be used to describe what is generously sufficient: *a*

generous serving; a liberal portion; a bountiful supply.
Antonyms: **cheap, stingy.**

genteel See **refined.**

gentle ***adj.*** **mild.**
GENTLE and MILD can be used interchangeably to describe people who are kindly, peaceful, and patient in disposition, manner, or behavior: *Gentle people can be brave. Jack's father was a mild man who rarely punished his children. Gentle* can also suggest a soothing quality (*gentle hands; gentle words; a gentle breeze*); *mild* describes what is moderate in degree, force, or effect (*a mild reproach; mild soap*).
Antonym: **harsh.**

genuine 1. See **natural. 2.** See **true. 3.** See **authentic.**

genuinely See **actually.**

germane See **relevant.**

get See **earn.**

ghastly ***adj.*** **grim, grisly, gruesome, horrible, horrid, lurid, macabre.**
Core meaning: Shockingly repellent (*the ghastly sight of starving refugees*).
2. cadaverous, deathly, spectral.
Core meaning: Gruesomely suggestive of ghosts or death (*the ghastly figure of the Headless Horseman; the ghastly pallor of the dying patient*).

gibe See **ridicule.**

gigantic See **big.**

gird See **surround.**

gist See **heart.**

glad ***adj.*** **cheerful, happy, joyful.**
These describe what shows, is marked by, or expresses pleasure, good spirits, delight, etc. HAPPY is the most general: *a happy fellow; a happy day.* CHEERFUL suggests evident high spirits: *a girl who is cheerful even in the morning;*

a cheerful face; a cheerful tune. GLAD suggests pleasure that a wish has been gratified (*The children were glad to get the skis they had hoped for*) or satisfaction with immediate circumstances (*I am glad I found you*). JOYFUL, the strongest of these words, suggests extremely high spirits or a very strong sense of fulfillment or satisfaction: *felt joyful at the prospect of seeing him at last; a joyful smile.*
***Antonym:* sad.**

glare See **gaze.**

glaring See **flagrant.**

glee See **gaiety.**

glib ***adj.*** **facile, flip** (*Informal*), **glossy, slick.**
Core meaning: Marked by ready but often insincere or superficial discourse (*a glib denial*).

glide See **slide.**

gloomy ***adj.*** **1. dour, glum, morose.**
All of these describe people who show a cheerless aspect or disposition. A GLOOMY person is by nature given to somberness or depression: *sullen and gloomy as he went about his tasks.* DOUR suggests a grim and humorless exterior: *a dour and ascetic minister.* GLUM often implies temporary low spirits: *When you are feeling glum, a talk with a friend can do a mountain of good.* MOROSE applies to those who are ill-humored and sullen: *a morose man who talked little with his neighbors.*
***Antonym:* cheerful.**
2. dismal, dreary.
GLOOMY, DISMAL, and DREARY describe what produces a feeling of melancholy or depression: *a gloomy, deserted castle; a dismal fog; a dreary January rain.*
***Antonym:* cheerful.**

glossy See **glib.**

glum See **gloomy.**

go See **operate.**

goad See **provoke.**

go-between ***n.*** **broker, intercessor, intermediary, intermediate, middleman.**
Core meaning: A person who acts as an intermediate agent in a transaction (*acted as the go-between in the labor dispute*).

godly See **holy.**

good-natured. See **amiable.**

goodness See **virtue.**

goods ***n.*** **commodities, line, merchandise, wares.**
Core meaning: Products bought and sold in commerce (*inventoried all the goods in the store*).

govern See **administer.**

grab See **catch.**

graceful ***adj.*** **1. adroit, deft, dexterous, nimble.**
Anything GRACEFUL shows beauty or charm of movement, form, or manner: *a graceful tango; a graceful figure; a graceful compliment*. The related words are more restricted in meaning. ADROIT, DEFT, DEXTEROUS, and NIMBLE apply to movement and manner. *Adroit* implies adeptness and skill, particularly under difficult conditions: *an adroit maneuver. Deft* suggests quickness, sureness, and lightness of touch: *a deft seamstress. Dexterous* applies to skilled manual activity: *a dexterous typist. Nimble* stresses quickness and liveliness in mental or physical performance: *nimble fingers*.
Antonym: **awkward.**
2. See **elegant.**

grand ***adj.*** **grandiose, imposing, magnificent, majestic, stately.**
GRAND and its synonyms apply to what is extremely impressive in some way. Both *grand* and MAGNIFICENT refer to what is fine, impressive, or splendid, as in appearance; *magnificent* especially suggests sumptuousness and excellence: *a grand coronation ceremony; a magnificent cathedral*. IMPOSING describes what is impressive with respect to size, bearing, power, etc.: *an imposing residence; an imposing officer*. STATELY refers mainly to what is impressive

in size or proportions: *stately columns; a stately oak.* MAJESTIC is applicable to manner, appearance, bearing, etc., and suggests dignity, nobility, or grandeur: *The queen gave a majestic wave of the hand.* GRANDIOSE refers principally to things that are on an exceedingly large scale (*a grandiose style of architecture*); in a related sense it often suggests pretentiousness, affectation, or pompousness (*full of grandiose ideas*).

grandiose See **grand.**

graphic ***adj.*** **lifelike, pictorial, realistic, vivid.**
Core meaning: Described verbally in accurate detail (*a graphic account of the battle*).

grasp See **comprehend.**

gratify See **please.**

gratifying See **pleasant.**

gratuitous ***adj.*** **supererogative, supererogatory, uncalled-for, wanton.**
Core meaning: Not required or warranted by the circumstances of the case (*gratuitous spending; the gratuitous killing of civilians by the conquering soldiers*).

gratuity See **bonus.**

great 1. See **big. 2.** See **excellent.**

grief See **sorrow.**

grim See **ghastly.**

grimy See **dirty.**

grin See **smile.**

grisly See **ghastly.**

gross 1. See **coarse. 2.** See **flagrant.**

grotesque See **fantastic.**

grown-up See **mature.**

gruesome See **ghastly.**

gruff *adj.* **bluff, blunt, brusque, curt.**
All of these adjectives refer to what is abrupt and sometimes markedly impolite in manner or speech. GRUFF implies roughness of manner and often harsh speech, but it does not necessarily suggest intentional rudeness. BRUSQUE emphasizes rude abruptness of manner. BLUNT stresses utter frankness and usually a disconcerting directness of speech. BLUFF refers to unpolished, unceremonious manner but usually implies good nature. CURT refers to briefness and abruptness of speech and manner and usually implies rudeness.

guard See **defend.**

guileful See **underhand.**

haggard *adj.* **careworn, wasted, worn.**
These adjectives describe what shows the effects of anxiety, disease, hunger, or fatigue. HAGGARD refers particularly to facial appearance and implies thinness, tiredness, and often the expression of one who has seemingly suffered or worried. CAREWORN is applicable to one whose physical appearance reveals the effects of worry, anxiety, or burdensome responsibility. WASTED stresses emaciation or marked loss of flesh, with consequent frailness or enfeeblement; the term is most often associated with illness or extreme physical hardship. WORN can refer to the effects of worry, sickness, or strain.

haggle See **argue.**

hale See **healthy.**

halt See **stop.**

hamper See **hinder.**

handicap See **disadvantage.**

handle *v.* **manipulate, ply, wield.**
These verbs refer to using, operating, or managing things or, less often, persons. HANDLE can refer to management or control of tools, implements, persons, or nonphysical things such as problems and situations; unless it is qualified

by an adverb, in every case the term suggests competence in gaining an end or objective. MANIPULATE connotes skillful or artful management of physical things, such as tools or instruments, or of persons or personal affairs, in which case it often implies deviousness. PLY refers principally to use of tools (*ply a broom in sweeping*) and to the regular and diligent engagement in a task (*ply the baker's trade*). WIELD implies that one has full command of what is used, principally tools and implements, weapons, means of expression such as the pen, or intangibles such as authority and influence.

handsome See **beautiful.**

handy See **convenient.**

hanging ***adj.*** **pendulous, pensile, suspended.**
Core meaning: Hung or appearing to be hung from a support (*a hanging plant*).

haphazard See **accidental.**

happy 1. See **cheerful. 2.** See **fortunate. 3.** See **glad.**

harangue See **tirade.**

hard ***adj.*** **firm.**
HARD and FIRM are often used interchangeably when they refer to what is resistant to pressure (*a hard surface; firm ground*). *Hard* can also suggest that something is physically toughened (*a hard palm with calluses*), while *firm* describes what shows the tone and resiliency characteristic of healthy tissue (*firm muscles*). See also **difficult.**
Antonym: **soft.**

harm ***n.*** **damage, detriment, hurt, injury.**
Core meaning: The action or result of inflicting loss or pain (*did harm to the hostages*).

harmony ***n.*** **accord, concord.**
These denote a condition marked by agreement in feeling, approach, action, disposition, etc.: *a community in perfect harmony; ideas in accord with my own; lived in peace and concord.*
Antonym: **discord.**

harsh ***adj.*** **rough, severe, stern.**
HARSH and its synonyms describe behavior, actions, etc., that affect the feelings unpleasantly or offensively: *a harsh remark; rough treatment; a severe tone of voice; a stern look of reproach. Harsh* and *rough* also apply to what is unpleasant to the senses: *harsh colors; rough wool. Severe* and *stern* can suggest that something is strict and inflexible: *a severe law; a severe teacher; stern discipline; a stern mother.*
Antonym: **gentle.**

harshness See **severity.**

hasten See **expedite.**

hasty See **fast.**

hate 1. ***n.*** **abhorrence, detestation, hatred, loathing.**
These nouns refer to intense feelings of dislike. HATE is often used as the abstract term: *Love and hate are opposites.* HATRED frequently refers more directly to the emotion as people experience it: *a hatred of liars.* For the differences in the meanings of the words ABHORRENCE, DETESTATION, and LOATHING, see the discussion below of the verbs from which they derive.
Antonym: **love.**
2. ***v.*** **abhor, detest, loathe.**
HATE, the most general of these terms, implies a feeling of aversion, enmity, or hostility: *"I hate you," he screamed at her.* ABHOR suggests a feeling of repugnance and even fear: *abhor violence in all forms.* DETEST and LOATHE imply intense dislike and scorn: *detest* (or *loathe*) *spinach; loathe* (or *detest*) *cheating.*
Antonym: **love.**

hatred See **hate.**

haughty See **proud.**

have See **carry.**

hazard See **danger.**

hazy See **vague.**

head See **administer.**

headstrong See **obstinate.**

healthy ***adj.*** **hale, sound, well.**

These adjectives describe persons who are in good physical or mental condition. WELL simply specifies the absence of disease: *He was sick for three days, but he is well now.* HEALTHY positively stresses a condition of good health and often suggests energy: *a healthy boy with a healthy appetite.* HALE stresses absence of infirmity, especially in elderly persons: *My grandmother is still hale and hearty.* SOUND emphasizes freedom from defect, decay, damage, injury, or sickness: *a sound mind in a sound body.*

Antonym: **sick.**

heart ***n.*** **core, essence, gist, kernel, marrow, nub, pith, root, substance.**

Core meaning: The most central and material part (*the heart of the matter*).

heartache See **sorrow.**

hearten See **encourage.**

heave See **raise.**

heavy ***adj.*** **cumbersome, hefty, massive, ponderous, weighty.**

HEAVY and its synonyms refer to what is of great or relatively great weight, size, etc. *Heavy* applies to what has great weight (*a heavy stone*); figuratively it describes what is burdensome or oppressive to the spirit: *heavy losses.* CUMBERSOME stresses difficulty of movement or operation caused by heaviness or bulkiness: *cumbersome luggage.* HEFTY refers mainly to heaviness or brawniness of physique: *a hefty sailor.* MASSIVE describes what is imposing in size (*a massive head*) or bulk (*a massive elephant*). PONDEROUS refers to what has great mass and weight and usually implies clumsiness: *ponderous prehistoric beasts.* WEIGHTY literally denotes having great weight (*a weighty package*); figuratively it describes what is very serious or important: *a weighty problem; a weighty decision.*

Antonym: light.

hedge See **skirt.**

heed See **notice.**

heedless See **careless.**

hefty See **heavy.**

help *v.* **aid, assist.**

These share the sense of contributing to the fulfillment of a need or the achievement of a purpose. HELP and AID are the most general: *helped with the farming; aids a friend in distress.* Sometimes *help* conveys a stronger suggestion of effective action: *Food helps the hungry more than advice on how to find work.* ASSIST usually implies making a lesser contribution or acting as a subordinate: *A crack team of trained guerrillas assisted the commander.*
Antonym: **hinder.**

helpless See **powerless.**

hem in See **surround.**

hesitate *v.* **falter, vacillate, waver.**

These verbs are used to express uncertainty or indecision. HESITATE implies slowness to act, speak, or decide. To FALTER is to act indecisively or ineffectually; it implies retreat from a course decided on or the inability to carry it out. VACILLATE implies swinging between alternative and often conflicting courses of action without making a decisive choice. WAVER suggests either inability to act, resulting from indecision, or tentative and ineffectual action once a choice has been made.
Antonym: **decide.**

heterogeneity See **variety.**

hide *v.* **cloak, conceal, secrete.**

These verbs refer to keeping from the sight or knowledge of others. HIDE and CONCEAL refer both to putting physical things out of sight (*hid the Christmas gifts in the closet; concealed the box under the bed*) and to withholding information or disguising one's feelings or thoughts (*hid the bad news; smiled and joked to conceal her hurt feelings*). *Con-*

ceal often implies a deliberate effort to keep from sight or knowledge, whereas *hide* also can refer to natural phenomena: *The thief hid* (or *concealed*) *the stolen money. Night hides the city's ugliness.* CLOAK usually refers to concealing thoughts, plans, etc.: *research cloaked in secrecy.* SECRETE refers chiefly to removing physical objects from sight and involves concealment in a place unknown to others: *secreted the money in a mattress.*
Antonym: **show.**

hideous See **ugly.**

high ***adj.*** **elevated, lofty, tall, towering.**
These refer to what stands out or is otherwise distinguished by reason of height. HIGH and TALL, the most general terms, are sometimes interchangeable. In general *high* refers to what rises a considerable distance from a base or is situated at a level well above another level considered as a base: *a high mountain; a high ceiling; a high shelf; high standards. Tall* describes what rises to a considerable extent; it often refers to living things and to what has great height in relation to breadth or in comparison with like things: *a tall man; tall trees; a tall building.* ELEVATED stresses height in relation to immediate surroundings; it refers principally to being raised or situated above a normal or average level (*an elevated plain*) but can also apply to something that is exalted in character or spirit (*elevated praise; elevated thought*). LOFTY describes what is imposingly or inspiringly high: *lofty mountains; lofty sentiments.* TOWERING suggests height that causes awe: *towering icebergs.*
Antonym: **low.**

hilarity See **gaiety.**

hinder ***v.*** **block, hamper, impede, obstruct.**
All of these share the sense of interfering with or preventing action or progress. HINDER and HAMPER are the most general; they apply to any restraining influence: *Diffidence hindered his ability to express himself. Rain hindered highway construction. Economic problems hamper the nation's de-*

velopment. Tight shoes hampered his freedom of movement. BLOCK and OBSTRUCT imply the setting up of obstacles: *The senator blocked passage of the bill for a week by filibustering. Guards blocked his entry. By withholding the documents the politician obstructed justice. Rocks obstructed the mountain pass.* To IMPEDE is to retard action or progress or make it so difficult that it is impossible: *Illogical thinking impedes the solution of geometry problems. Snow impeded the flow of traffic.*
Antonyms: **advance; help.**

hint 1. See **suggest. 2.** See **trace.**

hit *v.* **bash** (*Informal*), **belt** (*Informal*), **clip** (*Informal*), **clobber** (*Slang*), **paste** (*Slang*), **slam, slug** (*Slang*), **smack, smash, sock** (*Slang*), **strike, swat, wallop** (*Informal*), **whack.**
Core meaning: To deliver (a powerful blow) suddenly and sharply (*hit the other boxer in the jaw*).

hoard See **save.**

hoist See **raise.**

holding(s) *n.* **estate, possessions, property.**
Core meaning: Something, as land, legally possessed (*a company with vast holdings in South America*).

holocaust See **disaster.**

holy *adj.* **devout, godly, pious, religious.**
Core meaning: Concerned with God and religion (*a holy shrine*).

homage See **honor.**

honest See **true.**

honesty *n.* **honor, integrity, probity, veracity.**
HONESTY and its synonyms denote qualities closely associated with moral excellence. *Honesty* implies truthfulness (*Few doubted the President's honesty*), fairness in dealing (*treated his employees with absolute honesty*), and absence of fraud, deceit, and dissembling (*a banker of impeccable honesty*). HONOR suggests close adherence to a strict moral

or ethical code: *bound by his honor and his conscience.* INTEGRITY refers especially to moral soundness in individuals: *a man of integrity who never violated a trust.* PROBITY is proven integrity. VERACITY is truthfulness in expression: *doubted the veracity of the witness.*
***Antonym:* dishonesty.**

honor *n.* deference, homage, reverence, veneration.
These are compared as they refer to the state, feeling, or expression of admiration, respect, or esteem. HONOR, the most general, applies both to the feeling (*hold in honor*) and to the expression (*displaying the flag to show honor to the United States*). DEFERENCE is respect or courteous regard that often takes the form of yielding to the wishes, judgment, condition, etc., of another: *In deference to his age he was permitted to remain seated.* HOMAGE is a public expression of high regard or respect: *paid homage to his king; a crowd cheering in homage to a great singer.* REVERENCE is a feeling of deep respect and devotion and often of love: *gazed at the cathedral with reverence.* VENERATION is both the feeling and worshipful expression of respect, love, and awe, especially for one whose wisdom, dignity, rank, age, etc., merits such attention: *viewed his great-grandfather with veneration.* See also **honesty.**
***Antonym:* dishonor.**

honorable See **moral.**

hopeful See **optimistic.**

horizon See **ken.**

horrible See **ghastly.**

horrid See **ghastly.**

hostile See **unfriendly.**

hostility See **enmity.**

hot *adj.* boiling, burning, feverish, fiery, scorching, sizzling, sultry, sweltering, torrid.
Used literally, these words describe what has a high temperature; most of them also have figurative senses. HOT

applies most widely; its extended senses also describe what is warmer than usual (*a hot forehead*), highly spiced (*hot mustard*), or explosive or dangerous (*a hot dispute*). What is BOILING is heated to the boiling point (*boiling water*) or greatly excited, as with rage (*still boiling after their nasty fight*). BURNING calls up the image of fire; it refers to what is passionate (*a burning desire*) or urgent (*a burning issue*). FEVERISH suggests an abnormally high body temperature (*a feverish forehead*); it also applies to what is very active (*a feverish desire to win*). FIERY implies great heat, as of fire (*the fiery pavements of the city*); it can also describe what is high-spirited (*a fiery speech*) or easily stirred up (*a fiery temper*). SCORCHING applies literally to what is intensely hot (*a scorching summer day*) or figuratively to what is censorious or angry (*a scorching indictment of graft at city hall*). What is SIZZLING is so hot that it almost suggests the hissing sound characteristic of frying fat (*a tar sidewalk sizzling in the sun*); figuratively *sizzling* applies to something seething with anger or indignation (*sent a sizzling reply*). SULTRY means hot and humid (*a sultry day in August*); figuratively it refers to what is sensual and voluptuous (*gave him a sultry look*). SWELTERING, which implies oppressive and humid heat, has no figurative sense: *a sweltering apartment*. TORRID refers to what is very dry and hot (*torrid weather*) or to what is passionate (*a torrid romance*).
Antonym: **cold.**

huge See **big.**

human ***adj.*** **humane, humanitarian.**
These reflect concern with the welfare of people and the easing of suffering (*the alleviation of poverty—a human concern*). HUMAN is essentially a classifying term relating to individuals or people collectively (*human kindness*), while HUMANE stresses the qualities of kindness and compassion (*humane treatment*). HUMANITARIAN applies to what actively promotes the needs and welfare of people (*humanitarian considerations in the treatment of prisoners*).

humane See **human.**

humanitarian See **human.**

humble ***adj.*** **lowly, meek, modest.**

These refer mainly to demeanor or behavior. HUMBLE stresses lack of pride, assertiveness, or pretense: *my humble opinion.* MEEK implies patience, humility, and gentleness; it sometimes suggests that a person is easily imposed upon: *a meek and dignified manner; the meekest of men.* LOWLY combines the senses of *humble* and *meek: a lowly beggar child.* MODEST implies lack of vanity, pretension, or forwardness: *modest despite his fame.*

Antonym: **proud.**

humdrum See **monotony.**

humor See **pamper.**

hurt 1. See **distress. 2.** See **harm.**

husband See **save.**

hypothesis See **theory.**

icy See **cold.**

idea See **feeling.**

ideal 1. ***n.*** **model, standard.**

IDEAL and the other two nouns refer to what serves as the basis of direction or guidance in work or behavior. An *ideal* is a goal of perfection in the form of a person or thing: *found his ideal in the playing of Rubinstein.* A MODEL is a person or thing imitated or worthy of imitation: *a model of honesty.* A STANDARD is an established criterion or prevailing level of quality, value, or achievement that is demanded or aimed for: *an artist who set high standards for herself.*

2. ***adj.*** See **idealistic.**

idealistic ***adj.*** **1. ideal, utopian, visionary.**

Core meaning: Tending to envision things in a perfect but unrealistic form (*an idealistic attitude toward foreign affairs*).

2. quixotic, romantic, unrealistic.

Core meaning: Not compatible with reality (*an idealistic view of love*).

identical See **same.**

idiom See **language.**

idiosyncrasy See **eccentricity.**

idle See **inactive.**

ignite *v.* **kindle, light.**
These verbs mean to set fire to or catch fire: *ignite a match; a match that ignited; kindle a campfire; wood that kindles easily; light an oven; an oven that wouldn't light.*
Antonym: **extinguish.**

ignominy See **dishonor.**

ignorant *adj.* **illiterate, uneducated.**
Core meaning: Without education or knowledge (*ignorant teens who had quit school*).

ilk See **type.**

ill See **sick.**

illegal *adj.* **illegitimate, illicit, unlawful.**
All of these describe what conflicts with the law. ILLEGAL applies to what is prohibited by law or by official rules: *illegal gambling; an illegal move in a chess game.* ILLICIT stresses violation of accepted custom: *illicit relations.* ILLEGITIMATE describes what is not supported by the law: *an illegitimate deed to the property: illegitimate claims.* UNLAWFUL applies most often to what violates the law: *the unlawful possession of firearms.*
Antonym: **legal.**

illegitimate See **illegal.**

illicit See **illegal.**

illiterate See **ignorant.**

illogical **1.** See **fallacious.** **2.** See **unreasonable.**

imagination *n.* **fancy, fantasy.**
IMAGINATION, FANCY, and FANTASY refer to the ability of the mind to conceive ideas or to form images of something not present to the senses or within the actual experience of the

person involved. *Imagination* is broadly applicable to all such functions; it also applies to the creative use of that ability (*the lively imagination of the novelist*). *Fancy* suggests mental invention that is capricious, whimsical, or playful: *fact and fancy*. *Fantasy* is applied mainly to creative imagination (*Modern technology has turned fantasy into reality*) and to what exists only in the mind or imagination (*dismissed the idea as sheer fantasy*).

imbibe See **absorb.**

imitate *v.* **burlesque, mimic, parody.**
Core meaning: To copy (the manner or expression of another), often mockingly (*a comedian who imitated the President*).

immaculate See **clean.**

immaterial See **irrelevant.**

immature *adj.* **childish, infantile.**
These apply to what is thoughtless or foolish in a manner not suitable for a mature person: *an immature attitude toward work; childish, sulky behavior; an infantile outburst of rage.*
Antonym: **mature.**

immense See **big.**

immobile See **motionless.**

immoral *adj.* **1. unethical, unprincipled, unscrupulous.**
These describe that which is contrary to what is considered just, right, or good: *the immoral system of slavery; an unethical businessman; an unprincipled scoundrel; an unscrupulous politician.*
Antonym: **moral.**
2. dissolute, lecherous, lewd, profligate.
All of these apply to that which does not conform to accepted rules of propriety and morality in sexual matters. IMMORAL is the most general: *an immoral man; immoral behavior*. DISSOLUTE suggests moral corruption: *a dissolute life*. LECHEROUS and LEWD both imply a preoccupation with sexual desire and activity: *a lecherous glance; a lewd sug-*

gestion. PROFLIGATE, the strongest, means "completely given over to self-indulgence and vice."
Antonym: **moral.**

immorality See **vice.**

immortalize ***v.*** **eternalize, perpetuate.**
Core meaning: To cause to last forever (*immortalize her memory*).

impalpable See **imperceptible.**

impartial See **fair.**

impartially See **fairly.**

impatient ***adj.*** **restive.**
IMPATIENT applies to unwillingness or inability to wait patiently, endure irritation calmly, or show tolerant understanding: *impatient at the delay in the train's departure; a teacher impatient because Bill learned slowly.* RESTIVE applies more narrowly to impatience under restriction, pressure, or delay: *The crowd gradually grew restive while they waited for the speaker to appear.*
Antonym: **patient.**

impeach See **accuse.**

impeccable See **perfect.**

impede See **hinder.**

impel See **provoke.**

imperceptible ***adj.*** **impalpable, inappreciable, intangible.**
These adjectives describe what cannot—or can barely—be seen, measured, or detected by the senses or the mind even though it is present: *an imperceptible movement of her hand; an impalpable difference in meaning; an inappreciable amount; an intangible change.*
Antonym: **perceptible.**

imperfect ***adj.*** **defective, faulty.**
These describe what has defects, flaws, errors, etc.; they

can be used interchangeably: *imperfect speech; defective merchandise; a faulty memory.*
***Antonym:* perfect.**

imperious See **dictatorial.**

implausible ***adj.*** **flimsy, improbable, inconceivable, unbelievable, weak.**
Core meaning: Not plausible or believable (*an implausible alibi*).

implement 1. ***v.*** See **fulfill. 2.** ***n.*** See **tool.**

implicit ***adj.*** **implied, tacit.**
What is IMPLICIT is understood without being directly expressed: *The author's opposition to the war is implicit throughout the book.* IMPLIED and TACIT describe what is conveyed indirectly or suggested without being spoken or written: *an implied consent; a tacit agreement.*
***Antonym:* explicit.**

implied See **implicit.**

imply See **suggest.**

impolite ***adj.*** **discourteous, rude, unmannerly.**
These refer to lack of good behavior or manners. What is RUDE is offensive to the feelings of others; the word often connotes insolence: *apologized for his rude remarks.* IMPOLITE and DISCOURTEOUS imply lack of good manners and consideration for others: *too impolite to stand up when his grandmother came into the room; a discourteous guest who came for dinner two hours late.* UNMANNERLY suggests bad manners: *unmannerly behavior.*
***Antonym:* polite.**

impolitic See **tactless.**

important ***adj.*** **consequential, momentous, significant, weighty.**
These all refer to what is able to determine or change the course of events or the nature of things. IMPORTANT is the most general term: *an important seaport; an important*

message; an important crop; an important composer. CONSEQUENTIAL describes what is important because of its possible outcome, result, etc.: *a consequential blunder.* What is MOMENTOUS is of the utmost importance or significance: *a momentous occasion; a momentous discovery.* SIGNIFICANT applies to what is notable or adds important meaning: *a significant battle; a significant look.* WEIGHTY implies great seriousness: *a weighty decision.*

***Antonym:* unimportant.**

imposing See **grand.**

impossible ***adj.*** **impracticable, impractical, unattainable, unfeasible, unrealizable, unthinkable, unworkable.**

Core meaning: Not capable of happening or being done (*impossible dreams; an impossible plan*).

impostor ***n.*** **charlatan, faker, quack.**

IMPOSTOR and its synonyms denote persons who pretend to be other than what they are or who otherwise practice deception for gain. An *impostor* assumes the identity of another person for the purpose of deceiving. A CHARLATAN falsely claims to have expert skill or knowledge in a particular subject or field of activity. FAKER often refers to a person who perpetrates a fraud. A QUACK usually practices medicine without being qualified.

impotent See **powerless.**

impoverished See **poor.**

impracticable See **impossible.**

impractical See **impossible.**

impress See **affect.**

impression See **feeling.**

improbable 1. See **unlikely. 2.** See **implausible.**

improper See **unsuitable.**

improvise ***v.*** **ad-lib** (*Informal*), **extemporize, fake** (*Slang*), **make up.**

Core meaning: To compose or do without preparation (*improvise a speech*).

impudent See **bold.**

impure ***adj.*** **contaminated, polluted, unclean.**
Core meaning: Rendered unfit by the addition of other substances (*impure drinking water*).

impute See **attribute.**

inaccurate See **false.**

inactive ***adj.*** **dormant, idle, inert, lazy.**
These all mean not involved in or disposed to action or movement. INACTIVE implies neither a favorable nor an unfavorable judgment: *an inactive attorney.* DORMANT refers chiefly to states of suspended activity but often implies the possibility of renewal: *a dormant snake in its winter hideaway.* IDLE refers to inactivity of persons, whether or not through choice (*employees idle because of the strike; idle boys who refuse to study*). When it comes about by choice and a negative judgment is implied, LAZY is more accurate: *too lazy to write a thank-you note.* INERT implies lethargy, especially of mind or spirit.

inadvertent See **careless.**

inappreciable See **imperceptible.**

inappropriate See **unsuitable.**

inapt See **unsuitable.**

inaugural See **first.**

incapable See **unable.**

incentive See **stimulus.**

inception See **origin.**

incite See **provoke.**

incline See **dispose.**

incompetent See **unable.**

inconceivable See **implausible.**

inconsequential See **unimportant.**

inconstant See **capricious.**

incorrect See **false.**

increase *v.* **augment, enlarge.**

These verbs share the meaning of becoming or causing to become greater, as in size, extent, or quantity. INCREASE has the greatest range of meanings. Used intransitively it suggests steady growth: *Her salary increased yearly. The mayor's political influence increased.* In transitive use *increase* does not necessarily connote such progressive growth; it can imply addition in any respect: *The director increased her salary. Illness increased his depression.* AUGMENT usually applies to what is already developed or well under way: *sadness that augments with every visit to the hospital; augmented his collection of books.* ENLARGE implies expansion, physical or other: *The landowner enlarged his property by repeated purchases. Fran's group of friends enlarged by leaps and bounds.*

Antonym: **decrease.**

incredible See fabulous.

incurious See **uninterested.**

indeed See **actually.**

indefinite See **vague.**

indelicate 1. See **coarse. 2.** See **tactless.**

indescribable See **unspeakable.**

indication See **sign.**

indict See **accuse.**

indifference See **disinterest.**

indifferent See **uninterested.**

indigenous See **native.**

indigent See **poor.**

indignation See **anger.**

indirect *adj.* **circuitous, roundabout.**

These describe what does not go straight to its destination: *an indirect path; a circuitous route home; a roundabout course that avoided heavy traffic.* They are all used figuratively as well, in the meaning "not straight to the point." *Indirect* is the most general: *an indirect answer. Circuitous* and *roundabout* often imply an effort to evade or deceive.

Antonym: **direct.**

indispensable See **necessary.**

indisposed See **sick.**

indistinct See **vague.**

individual 1. See **characteristic. 2.** See **single.**

indulge See **pamper.**

industry See **business.**

inebriated See **drunk.**

inept See **awkward.**

inequitable See **unfair.**

inert See **inactive.**

inessential See **unnecessary.**

inestimable See **valuable.**

inexpensive See **cheap.**

infamous See **outrageous.**

infamy See **dishonor.**

infantile See **immature.**

inferior See **minor.**

infirmity See **weakness.**

inflame See **provoke.**

inflexible ***adj.*** **rigid, stiff.**

These three adjectives describe what literally is difficult to bend or stretch and to human behavior and attitudes that are not subject to modification or change. Anything STIFF cannot easily be bent (*a stiff board*); in reference to persons *stiff* suggests firmness of position and either lack of ease in manner or cold formality (*behavior that became stiff when*

she met new people; very stiff and proud around the children). INFLEXIBLE and RIGID refer to what cannot be bent physically, at least without damage or deformation (*an inflexible piece of steel; a rigid iron frame*); figuratively they describe unyielding positions or attitudes: *an inflexible rule; a rigid social structure; inflexible* (or *rigid*) *in his demands.*
Antonym: **flexible.**

influence See **affect.**

informal ***adj.*** **casual**
These two adjectives describe what is not bound to or does not follow set ceremonies, rules, or conventions: *an informal agreement; an informal invitation; addressing his friends in a casual way; a casual survey.*
Antonym: **formal.**

information See **knowledge.**

infraction See **breach.**

infringement See **breach.**

inhuman See **cruel.**

initial See **first.**

initiate See **begin.**

initiative See **ambition.**

injury See **harm.**

inquisitive See **curious.**

insanity ***n.*** **dementia, lunacy, madness, mania.**
All these terms denote conditions of mental disability. INSANITY, a social and legal term, is a serious and often prolonged condition of mental illness or disorder that renders a person not legally responsible for his actions. DEMENTIA implies mental deterioration brought on by organic disorders. LUNACY is sometimes used interchangeably with *insanity*. MADNESS, a more general term, often stresses the violent side of mental illness. MANIA refers mainly to the excited phase of manic-depressive psychosis.
Antonym: **sanity.**

insensible See **apathetic.**

insignificant See **unimportant.**

insinuate See **suggest.**

inspection See **analysis.**

instability ***n.*** **precariousness, shakiness, unsteadiness.**
Core meaning: The quality or condition of being undependable and erratic (*the current instability of the stock market*).

instant See **moment.**

instinctive See **involuntary.**

instruct 1. See **command. 2.** See **teach.**

instrument 1. See **means. 2.** See **tool.**

insubordinate See **rebellious.**

insufficiency See **deficiency.**

insult See **offend.**

insurrection See **rebellion.**

intangible See **imperceptible.**

integrity See **honesty.**

intellectual See **intelligent.**

intelligent ***adj.*** **bright, brilliant, intellectual, smart.**
All of these refer to what has or shows the ability to learn, think, understand, or know. INTELLIGENT usually implies the ability to deal with demands created by novel situations and new problems, to apply what is learned from experience, and to use the power of reasoning effectively as a guide to behavior. BRIGHT, sometimes used interchangeably with *intelligent,* implies mental quickness in general; BRILLIANT suggests extreme and impressive intelligence. INTELLECTUAL stresses the working of the mind; *intellectual* persons show superior mental capacity. SMART is often a general term implying mental alertness; it can refer to practical knowledge or the ability to learn quickly.
Antonym: **unintelligent.**

intense ***adj.*** **deep, extreme.**
These describe what is of very great concentration, power, force, depth, etc.: *an intense blue; an intense light; a deep silence; a deep sleep; extreme caution; extreme cold.*

intentional ***adj.*** **deliberate, premeditated, voluntary.**
These adjectives describe what happens by plan or design. INTENTIONAL and DELIBERATE imply that something is done or said on purpose: *an intentional snub; a deliberate lie.* PREMEDITATED applies when one has planned on or thought out a course of action in advance: *premeditated murder.* VOLUNTARY describes action taken of one's own free will, without constraint: *a voluntary commitment to a cause.* See also **voluntary.**
Antonym: **accidental.**

intercessor See **go-between.**

interest ***n.*** **concern, curiosity.**
INTEREST and CONCERN refer to a feeling of involvement with or regard for something or someone: *The woman's father viewed her career with interest. The headlines triggered widespread concern among the public. Interest* and CURIOSITY agree in suggesting a desire to know or learn, in the case of *curiosity* often about something new or strange: *The beginning of the book failed to catch his interest. The articles about Laetrile sparked her curiosity.*
Antonym: **disinterest.**

interfere ***v.*** **meddle, tamper.**
INTERFERE, MEDDLE, and TAMPER are compared as they apply to concerning oneself in the affairs of others. *Interfere* and *meddle* are sometimes interchangeable. *Meddle* is the stronger in implying unwanted, unwarranted, or unnecessary intrusion: *meddling in matters that do not concern him.* It is somewhat weaker than *interfere* in implying action that seriously hampers, hinders, or frustrates: *interfered with her attempts to solve her personal problems. Tamper* refers to rash or harmful intervention: *tampered with his feelings.*

intermediary See **go-between.**

intermediate 1. ***n.*** See **go-between. 2.** ***adj.*** See **middle.**

intermittent See **discontinuous.**

intimate See **suggest.**

intimidate See **threaten.**

intoxicated See **drunk.**

intractable See **obstinate.**

intricate See **complex.**

intrigue See **conspiracy.**

introductory See **preliminary.**

intuition See **feeling.**

invalid ***adj.*** **1. null, void.**
INVALID, NULL, and VOID describe what is without legal force, foundation, effect, etc.: *an invalid will; a contract rendered null by a later agreement; declare a marriage null and void.*
Antonym: **valid.**
2. See **fallacious.**

invaluable See **valuable.**

invective See **abusive.**

inveigle See **seduce.**

invert See **reverse.**

invest See **wrap.**

investigation See **analysis.**

involuntary ***adj.*** **automatic, instinctive.**
These describe actions that are not based on conscious choice. INVOLUNTARY refers to what is not subject to the control of the will: *an involuntary muscle spasm.* What is AUTOMATIC is done or produced by the body without conscious control or awareness: *an automatic reflex in the face*

of danger. INSTINCTIVE actions are directed by unlearned inner drives: *The seasonal migration of birds is instinctive.*
***Antonym:* voluntary.**

involved See **complex.**

ire See **anger.**

irk See **annoy.**

ironic See **sarcastic.**

irrational See **unreasonable.**

irregular See **abnormal.**

irrelevant ***adj.*** **immaterial.**
IRRELEVANT and IMMATERIAL describe what has no relation to a subject or situation at hand: *We must stick to our subject and avoid irrelevant digressions. Immaterial* often suggests that something is unimportant: *If you aren't in the right place at the right time, your qualifications usually turn out to be immaterial.*
***Antonym:* relevant.**

irreverent See **disrespectful.**

irreversible See **irrevocable.**

irrevocable ***adj.*** **irreversible, unalterable.**
Core meaning: That cannot be revoked or undone (*an irrevocable decision*).

irritate See **annoy.**

isolated See **secluded.**

isolation 1. See **solitude. 2.** See **aloneness.**

issue See **effect.**

iteration See **repetition.**

jeremiad See **tirade.**

jest See **joke.**

jiffy See **moment.**

job See **work.**

join ***v.*** **connect, link, unite.**
JOIN and its synonyms denote bringing or coming together. *Join* has the widest application, in both literal and figurative use: *join hands; join the ends of a chain; join in wedlock.* CONNECT and LINK imply a looser relationship in which individual units retain their identity while coming together at some point: *Capillaries connect the arteries and the veins. The Panama Canal links the Atlantic and the Pacific.* UNITE stresses the coherence or oneness that results from joining: *a plan to unite the colonies under one government; uniting for peace.*
Antonym: **separate.**

joke ***n.*** **crack, gag, jest, quip, sally, wisecrack, witticism.**
These refer to forms of humorous sayings or actions. JOKE and JEST, which can denote something said or done, are approximately interchangeable, though *jest* occurs infrequently in this sense. A WITTICISM is a cleverly worded, amusing remark. QUIP suggests a light, pointed, bantering remark, and SALLY a sudden, clever, or witty statement. CRACK and WISECRACK, informal terms, refer to flippant or sarcastic retorts. GAG, also informal, is principally applicable to a broadly comic remark.

joy ***n.*** **delight, enjoyment, pleasure.**
These terms denote states of happiness or satisfaction. DELIGHT applies to intense satisfaction: *The children opened their gifts with delight.* ENJOYMENT often suggests ongoing or sustained pleasure: *Books are a source of great enjoyment to him.* JOY implies an intense and sustained state and is often associated with self-realization, sharing, or high-mindedness: *the joy of cooking; the joys of motherhood.* PLEASURE is the least forceful of these terms; it often merely refers to a pleasant sensation, emotion, etc.: *She smiled with pleasure as she watched the robins build their nest.*
Antonym: **sorrow.**

joyful See **glad.**

judge ***n.*** **arbiter, arbitrator, referee, umpire.**
JUDGE and its synonyms denote persons empowered to make decisions that determine points at issue. A *judge* is

either the presiding officer in a court of justice or, in a nonlegal sense, anyone in a position to make decisions because he has authority or knowledge recognized as authoritative. An ARBITRATOR usually works, singly or with associates, to settle disputes, especially in labor-management relations, and derives his authority by advance consent of the parties to the dispute, who choose him or approve his selection for the job. An ARBITER is usually one who has no official status but is recognized as pre-eminent in a given nonlegal area, such as fashion or literature; less often, *arbiter* is used interchangeably with *arbitrator*. In legal terminology a REFEREE is an attorney appointed by a court to make a determination of a case or to investigate and report on it, and an UMPIRE is a person called upon to settle an issue that arbitrators are unable to resolve.

judgment See **opinion.**

judicious See **wise.**

just See **fair.**

justifiable ***adj.*** **defensible, excusable, tenable.**
Core meaning: Capable of being justified (*a justifiable reaction*).

justification See **explanation.**

justly See **fairly.**

juvenile See **young.**

keen See **sharp.**

ken ***n.*** **horizon, purview, range, reach, scope.**
Core meaning: The extent of one's understanding, knowledge, or vision (*written in technical language beyond my ken*).

kernel See **heart.**

kind 1. ***adj.*** **benevolent, compassionate, kindly.**
These describe persons and their actions when they show concern and sympathy for others. KIND and KINDLY are interchangeable when they describe persons and their na-

tures: *a kind man; a kindly, warm-hearted woman.* BENEVOLENT suggests charitableness and a desire to promote others' welfare: *a benevolent ruler.* A COMPASSIONATE person is quick to sense another's suffering and often feels a wish to help or show mercy.
Antonym: **unkind.**
2. ***n.*** See **type.**

kindle 1. See **ignite. 2.** See **provoke.**

kindly See **kind.**

kismet See **fate.**

knowledge ***n.*** **erudition, information, learning, scholarship.**
These nouns refer to what one acquires and retains through study and experience. KNOWLEDGE is the broadest; it includes facts and ideas (*technical knowledge*), understanding (*our knowledge of the universe*), and the totality of what is known (*value knowledge for its own sake*). ERUDITION implies profound knowledge, often in a specialized area: *a scholar's erudition.* INFORMATION suggests a collection of facts and data about a certain subject or event: *An encyclopedia is a good source of information.* LEARNING refers to what is gained by schooling and study: *men of learning.* SCHOLARSHIP is the mark of one who has mastered some area of learning, which is reflected in the scope, thoroughness, and care of his work.
Antonym: **ignorance.**

labor See **work.**

lack See **deficiency.**

laconic See **concise.**

land See **nation.**

language ***n.*** **1. dialect, speech, tongue, vernacular.**
Core meaning: A system of terms used by a people sharing a history and culture (*Polish and Russian—two Slavic languages*).
2. cant, idiom, jargon, lexicon, terminology, vocabulary.
Core meaning: Specialized expressions characteristic of a

field, subject, trade, or subculture (*the language of electrical engineering; street language*).

large See **big.**

last ***adj.*** **eventual, final, terminal, ultimate.**

LAST and its synonyms refer to what marks an end or conclusion. *Last* applies to what brings a series, sequence, or any collection of like things to an end: *the last day of the month; the last piece of candy.* FINAL refers to what comes at the end of a progression or process and stresses the definiteness of the conclusion: *his final remark; our final offer.* TERMINAL is applied to what marks an end, a limit, or a boundary, as in space, time, development, etc.: *the terminal point of enemy penetration; the terminal stage of cancer.* EVENTUAL refers to what will occur at an unspecified future time: *the eventual date of publication; the eventual downfall of a corrupt government.* ULTIMATE is applied to what marks the end of a lengthy progression beyond which there exists no other: *our ultimate fate; an ultimate goal; the ultimate authority.*

Antonym: **first.**

late ***adj.*** **overdue, tardy.**

These apply to what fails to appear or take place at the usual, expected, or proper time. OVERDUE suggests a failure to meet an obligation when due: *Your rent is overdue!* TARDY is generally applied to persons who show up after an appointed time: *a tardy guest.* LATE fits either sense: *late returning your library books; late for the party.*

Antonym: **early.**

latency See **abeyance.**

later ***adj.*** **after, subsequent.**

Core meaning: Following something else in time (*later developments proved his predictions*).

laughable ***adj.*** **comic, comical, funny, laughing, risible.**

Core meaning: Deserving laughter (*a laughable matter*).

laughing See **laughable.**

lavish See **luxurious.**

law *n.* **1. canon, edict, precept, rule.**
Core meaning: A principle governing political affairs (*the law of nations*).
2. axiom, principle, theorem, universal.
Core meaning: A basic rule or truth (*the laws of decency*).

lawful See **legal.**

lax See **loose.**

lazy See **inactive.**

league See **union.**

lean See **thin.**

learning See **knowledge.**

leave See **abandon.**

leave off See **stop.**

lecherous See **immoral.**

lecture See **speech.**

legal *adj.* **lawful, legitimate.**
These describe what is authorized, established, recognized, approved, or permitted by law. In this sense LEGAL and LAWFUL are often interchangeable: *legal* (or *lawful*) *activities; his legal* (or *lawful*) *wife*. LEGITIMATE refers to what is in accordance with the law (*a legitimate political regime*), but it also applies to what is reasonable (*a legitimate reason for leaving*) and to what is authentic and genuine (*a legitimate complaint*).
Antonym: **illegal.**

legitimate See **legal.**

leisurely See **slow.**

lend *v.* **loan.**
To LEND is to give or allow the use of something temporarily on the condition that it—or its equivalent in kind—be returned (*lend a book*); it may also mean putting at another's disposal something that cannot be returned, as, for example, time or talent (*lend assistance*). LOAN is a synonym

of *lend* only in the first sense; in a financial transaction the payment of interest is usually implied.
Antonym: **borrow.**

lengthy See **long.**

lessen See **decrease.**

lesser See **minor.**

let See **permit.**

letdown See **disappointment.**

lethal See **fatal.**

lethargic See **apathetic.**

level ***adj.*** **even, flat, flush, plane, smooth.**
All of these apply to surfaces in which there are no, or no significant, variations in the form of elevations or depressions. LEVEL implies being horizontal or parallel with the line of the horizon: *level farmland.* FLAT often—but not always—refers to such a horizontal surface: *a flat geometric figure; a flat dish.* EVEN and PLANE refer to flat surfaces that are without elevations or depressions: *an even board; a plane figure.* FLUSH applies to a surface that is on an exact level with an adjoining one, forming a continuous surface: *a door that is flush with the wall.* SMOOTH describes a surface in which the absence of even slight irregularities can be established by sight or touch: *smooth wood; a smooth skin.*

lewd See **immoral.**

lexicon See **language.**

liable ***adj.*** **accountable, answerable, responsible.**
Core meaning: Legally obligated (*parents are liable for vandalism done by their children*).

liberal See **generous.**

liberate See **free.**

liberty See **freedom.**

license 1. See **freedom.** 2. See **permission.**

lie ***n.*** **falsehood, falsity, fib, fiction, story, tale, untruth.**
Core meaning: An untrue declaration (*spread lies about the senator's personal life*).

lifeless See **dead.**

lifelike See **graphic.**

lift See **raise.**

light 1. See **easy. 2.** See **ignite.**

lighthearted See **cheerful.**

like ***v.*** **dote, enjoy, fancy, relish.**
LIKE and its synonyms mean to be attracted to or take pleasure in. *Like,* the least forceful, usually suggests only mild interest or regard: *She liked Jim a great deal but not enough to spend every evening with him.* DOTE (always used with *on*) implies foolish and extravagant attachment: *a woman who doted on her granddaughter.* ENJOY is applied to what gives pleasure (*enjoyed the movie*) or fulfillment (*enjoys living in the country*); FANCY, to what appeals to one's taste, inclination, caprice, etc. (*didn't fancy chocolates*); and RELISH, to what moves one to keen or zestful appreciation (*relished compliments*).
Antonym: **dislike.**

likely ***adj.*** **probable.**
LIKELY and PROBABLE refer to what shows a strong probability of happening or of being true: *It is likely to rain at any moment. Carelessness was the probable cause of the accident.* Both also describe what seems to be true but is not certain: *a likely excuse; a probable explanation.*
Antonym: **unlikely.**

limit ***v.*** **circumscribe, delimit, restrict.**
Core meaning: To specify the greatest amount or number allowed (*limited the number of free passes*).

line See **goods.**

lingering See **chronic.**

link See **join.**

listless See **apathetic.**

little ***adj*****. diminutive, miniature, minute, small, tiny.**
LITTLE and its synonyms all apply to what is not large in size. *Little* is the most general and is often used interchangeably with SMALL. DIMINUTIVE, MINUTE, and TINY suggest that which is of extremely small size. MINIATURE can also be used loosely to mean "exceedingly small" but strictly refers to something that is on a scale greatly reduced from the usual.
Antonym: **big.**

live See **alive.**

livelihood See **living.**

liveliness See **spirit.**

lively See **active.**

living ***n*****. livelihood, maintenance, subsistence, support.**
LIVING and its synonyms refer to what provides the necessities of life. *Living* and LIVELIHOOD often specify the occupation, work, or other means by which one earns his income: *Eskimos make their living by hunting and trapping. Jackson practiced medicine as a livelihood.* SUBSISTENCE often refers to what barely supports life: *earned his daily subsistence from the soil.* MAINTENANCE and SUPPORT are usually reckoned as the equivalent in money of what is needed for necessities such as food, lodging, and clothing: *a divorced man who provides maintenance* (or *support*) *for his family.* See also **alive.**

load See **charge.**

loan See **lend.**

loathe See **hate.**

loathing See **hate.**

locality See **area.**

lofty See **high.**

logic ***n*****. ratiocination, rationality, reason.**
Core meaning: Exact, valid, and rational reasoning (*his logic was unassailable*).

logical See **sensible.**

lone See **alone.**

loneliness See **aloneness.**

lonely See **alone.**

loneness See **aloneness.**

lonesome See **alone.**

long ***adj.*** **extended, lengthy.**

LONG describes what has great length or is of relatively great duration or extent: *a long river; a long novel; a long wait; a long journey.* LENGTHY is often interchangeable with *long: a lengthy explanation; a lengthy journey.* What is EXTENDED continues for a long period of time: *extended peace talks.*

Antonym: **short.**

loose ***adj.*** **lax, slack.**

LOOSE and SLACK can be used interchangeably to refer to what is literally insufficiently stretched: *a loose* (or *slack*) *rope. Loose* also describes what is not tight-fitting (*a loose robe*), tightly fitted (*loose sleeves*), or tightly fastened (*loose shoelaces*). *Slack* and LAX suggest carelessness or negligence: *a slack performance; lax about paying bills.*

Antonym: **tight.**

lose ***v.*** **mislay.**

To LOSE is to fail to find in the usual place (*lost my dictionary*). To MISLAY is to put in a place that one cannot remember: *She mislaid her hat.*

Antonym: **find.**

lost See **vanished.**

lot See **fate.**

love 1. ***n.*** **affection, devotion, fondness.**

All of these refer to feelings of attraction and attachment experienced by persons. LOVE suggests an intense feeling: *a husband's love for his wife; love of reading.* AFFECTION is a steady feeling of warm regard: *motherly affection; an affec-*

tion for animals. DEVOTION is dedication, attachment, and loyalty to a person or thing: *his devotion to his mother; devotion to the cause.* FONDNESS, in its most common sense, is rather strong liking for a person or thing: *a fondness for his friends; a fondness for grapes.*

***Antonym:* hate.**

2. *v.* adore, cherish.

These all refer to feelings of love or strong affection. LOVE is the most neutral: *loved her husband; loves reading.* ADORE stresses devotion (*adored her mother*); used in an informal sense, it merely means "to like very much" (*adores skiing*). CHERISH emphasizes tender care: *The old man cherished the foundling as if she were his own. The collector cherishes his paintings.*

***Antonym:* hate.**

lovely See **beautiful.**

lower 1. *v.* drop.

To LOWER is to let, bring, or move something down to a lower level: *lowered her eyelids; lower the flag; lower your head.* To DROP is to let fall: *She dropped her glasses.*

***Antonym:* raise.**

2. *v.* cut, reduce, slash.

These words all mean to decrease, as in amount, value, etc. LOWER, CUT, and REDUCE are often interchangeable in this sense: *lowering taxes; cut prices; reduced costs.* SLASH implies great reduction: *slashed prices for the sale.*

***Antonym:* raise.**

3. *adj.* See **minor.**

lowly See **humble.**

loyal 1. See **faithful. 2.** See **true.**

lucky See **fortunate.**

ludicrous See **absurd.**

lunacy See **insanity.**

lure See **seduce.**

lurid See **ghastly.**

luscious See **delicious.**

lush See **luxurious.**

luxurious *adj.* **lavish, lush, luxuriant, opulent, palatial, plush, rich.**
Core meaning: Marked by extravagant, ostentatious magnificence (*a luxurious yacht*).

lying See **dishonesty.**

macabre See **ghastly.**

machination See **conspiracy.**

macrocosm See **universe.**

madness See **insanity.**

magnificent See **grand.**

magnitude See **bulk.**

maintenance See **living.**

majestic See **grand.**

make *v.* **1. construct, fabricate, fashion, manufacture, shape.**
Core meaning: To create by forming, combining, or altering materials (*made a house from logs; make a sandwich*).
2. See **constitute.**

make up 1. See **constitute. 2.** See **improvise.**

male *adj.* **manful, manly, mannish, masculine, virile.**
MALE and MASCULINE are essentially classifying terms. *Male* merely categorizes by sex; it is also applicable to animals, plants, and even things: *a male voice; a male rabbit; a male thread on a bolt. Masculine* can be used to categorize (*the masculine lead in a play*), but it can also describe traits, good and bad, considered characteristic of men: *masculine strength; masculine pride.* MANFUL and MANLY suggest such traits as braveness and resoluteness: *a manful* (or *manly*) *attempt.* MANNISH almost always indicates affectation of masculine traits or style by women: *a mannish haircut.* VIRILE stresses physical and sexual power.
***Antonym:* female.**

malevolent *adj.* **evil, malicious, malign, malignant, mean, nasty, poisonous, venomous, wicked.**
Core meaning: Marked by ill will and spite (*a malevolent hatred of his rival*).

malicious See **malevolent.**

malign See **malevolent.**

malignant See **malevolent.**

maltreat See **abuse.**

manage See **administer.**

managerial See **executive.**

mandatory See **compulsory.**

maneuver See **move.**

manful See **male.**

mania See **insanity.**

manipulate See **handle.**

manly See **male.**

manner See **method.**

mannerism See **affectation.**

manners *n.* **decorum, etiquette, proprieties.**
Core meaning: Socially correct behavior (*had to mind his manners at the party*).

mannish See **male.**

manufacture See **make.**

margin See **border.**

mark 1. See **sign. 2.** See **notice.**

markdown See **depreciation.**

market See **sell.**

marriage *n.* **matrimony, nuptials, wedding, wedlock.**
MARRIAGE is applied broadly to the state or process of being married, to the ceremony involved, and to any close union (*a marriage of minds; opera, a marriage of music and

drama). MATRIMONY applies to the condition of being married, often with emphasis on its religious nature. WEDLOCK pertains to the condition, primarily from a legal standpoint. WEDDING applies to the ceremony or celebrating, with connotations of social festivity. NUPTIALS applies most often to a wedding ceremony and may emphasize the religious aspect.

marrow See **heart.**

marvelous See **fabulous.**

masculine See **male.**

massive See **heavy.**

master See **professional.**

mastery See **expertise.**

material 1. See **relevant. 2.** See **matter.**

matrimony See **marriage.**

matter ***n.*** **material, stuff, substance.**
Core meaning: That from which things are made (*interesting matter for a novel*).

mature ***adj.*** **adult, grown-up.**
These apply to what has or shows the mental and emotional qualities associated with adults: *mature judgment; adult behavior; grown-up for her age.*
Antonym: **immature.**

maybe ***adv.*** **perchance, perhaps.**
Core meaning: Possibly but not certainly (*Maybe he'll come, and maybe not*).

mean See **malevolent.**

meaning ***n.*** **sense, significance, signification.**
MEANING is nonspecific and overlaps each of the following. SENSE, in this context, may be used to indicate the meaning conveyed by speech or writing (*Paragraphs often mark a break in the sense*) or to denote a particular meaning of a single word or phrase (*Words that are synonyms are usually alike in some senses*). SIGNIFICANCE stresses underlying or

long-range meaning; it implies evaluation: *a historical event of great significance.* SIGNIFICATION applies to accepted or established meaning, conveyed directly: *the dictionary signification of a word.*

means ***n.*** **agency, instrument, mechanism, medium.**
Core meaning: That by which something is accomplished (*increase sales by means of a new advertising campaign*).

measure See **move.**

mechanism See **means.**

meddle See **interfere.**

meditative See **pensive.**

medium See **means.**

meek See **humble.**

meet See **face.**

melancholy See **sad.**

melee See **conflict.**

menace See **threaten.**

mendacity See **dishonesty.**

mentality See **psychology.**

merchandise 1. See **sell.** 2. See **goods.**

mercurial See **capricious.**

merit See **earn.**

merriment See **gaiety.**

merrymaking See **gaiety.**

messy See **disorderly.**

method ***n.*** **fashion, manner, mode, system, way.**
These all refer to the procedures or plans followed to accomplish a given task. METHOD often suggests regularity of procedure; it emphasizes detailed, logically ordered plans: *Three methods of purifying water are to filter it, to distill it, and to add chemicals to it.* SYSTEM stresses order and regularity affecting all parts and details of a procedure: *a system*

for improving production. MANNER, FASHION, and MODE refer more to individual and distinctive procedure, as that dictated by preference, tradition, custom, etc.: *taught in an innovative manner; sings in an interesting fashion; an unusual mode of painting.* WAY is the most neutral and general of these terms and is often an inclusive synonym for them: *a better way of working out accounting problems.*

meticulous See **careful.**

mid See **middle.**

middle *adj.* **central, intermediate, mid, midway.**
Core meaning: Not extreme (*took the middle course in the negotiations*).

middleman See **go-between.**

midway See **middle.**

mild See **gentle.**

mimic See **imitate.**

mind 1. See **obey. 2.** See **psychology.**

miniature See **little.**

minimize See **belittle.**

minor *adj.* **inferior, lesser, lower, secondary.**
Core meaning: Of subordinate standing or importance (*a minor consideration*).

minus See **disadvantage.**

minute 1. See **little. 2.** See **moment.**

miraculous See **fabulous.**

mirth See **gaiety.**

miscarry See **fail.**

miserable See **sad.**

miserly See **stingy.**

misery See **distress.**

misgiving 1. See **doubt. 2.** See **qualm.**

mishandle See **botch.**

mislay See **lose.**

mislead See **deceive.**

mismanage See **botch.**

mistake See **error.**

mistreat See **abuse.**

mobile See **moving.**

mock See **ridicule.**

mode See **method.**

model See **ideal.**

modern *adj.* **contemporary, current, present-day.**
These all refer to what belongs to the moment in time intermediate between the past and the future: *modern life; a contemporary composer; current developments; present-day living.* MODERN can also stress a break with tradition and bold new experimentation and originality: *modern art; modern dance.*
Antonym: **old.**

modernize *v.* **refurbish, rejuvenate, restore, update.**
Core meaning: To make modern in appearance or style (*modernized the factory*).

modest 1. See **humble. 2.** See **plain. 3.** See **shy.**

modify See **change.**

mollify See **pacify.**

moment *n.* **flash, instant, jiffy, minute, second, trice.**
MOMENT pertains to a brief but usually not insignificant period; the sense of importance is strengthened when the term specifies a point in time: *a great moment in history.* MINUTE, used strictly, is specific; informally it is interchangeable with *moment: Wait a minute* (or *moment*). An INSTANT is a period of time almost too brief to detect; though the term is imprecise, it implies haste and usually urgency, especially as a specific point in time: *Come this instant!* SECOND may be used specifically or it may be used loosely, as

the equivalent of *instant* (*Come this second!*). TRICE, a literary term, and FLASH and the informal JIFFY appear in combinations preceded by *in a* (as *in a trice*—or *flash* or *jiffy*); they are imprecise but approximately equal in duration to *instant;* they imply haste but not necessarily urgency.

momentary See **temporary.**

momentous See **important.**

monkey See **fiddle.**

monotony ***n.*** **humdrum, tediousness, tedium.**
Core meaning: A tiresome lack of variety (*The monotony of office routine*).

monstrous See **outrageous.**

moral ***adj.*** **1. decent, ethical, honorable.**
These describe what conforms to accepted standards of what is considered just, right, or good: *made a moral choice; decent behavior; ethical business practices; an honorable man.*
Antonym: **immoral.**
2. chaste, pure, virtuous.
These four apply to what conforms to accepted rules of propriety and morality, especially in sexual matters: *moral behavior; a virtuous woman.* CHASTE and PURE often imply virginity or celibacy: *a chaste nun; a pure child.*
Antonym: **immoral.**

morality See **virtue.**

morose See **gloomy.**

mortal See **fatal.**

motionless ***adj.*** **immobile, still.**
These all apply to what is not in motion. MOTIONLESS is the most general: *stood motionless in front of his boss's desk.* IMMOBILE can refer to what is not moving (*paused immobile beside the tree*) or to what is fixed and not movable (*a statue immobile on its pedestal*). STILL implies lack of motion, noise, or disturbance: *still water; a still night.*
Antonym: **moving.**

motivate See **provoke.**

motivation See **stimulus.**

mount See **rise.**

movable See **moving.**

move 1. ***n.*** **maneuver, measure, procedure, step, tactic.**
Core meaning: An action calculated to achieve an end (*trying to decide their next move*).
2. ***v.*** See **affect.**
3. ***v.*** See **provoke.**

moving ***adj.*** **1. mobile, movable.**
MOVING applies to what changes or can change position: *a moving truck; moving parts.* What is MOBILE can move (*An animal's tail is mobile*) or be moved from place to place (*a mobile hospital*). MOVABLE implies only the capability of being moved: *movable type.*
Antonym: **motionless.**
2. affecting, pathetic, poignant, stirring, touching.
All of these refer to emotional reaction. MOVING applies to what calls forth any deeply felt emotion: *a moving love story.* STIRRING stresses strong emotion and is related to stimulation and inspiration: *a stirring anthem.* POIGNANT describes what is piercing or penetrating (*poignant criticism*); it also applies to what is keenly distressing or painful (*poignant grief*) and what appeals to the emotions (*poignant memories*). TOUCHING emphasizes sympathy and compassion: *a touching letter.* PATHETIC stresses pity (*a pathetic old woman*) and sometimes mild scorn for what is hopelessly inept or inadequate (*a pathetic attempt at humor*). AFFECTING applies to anything capable of moving the feelings but often pertains to what inspires pity and tenderness: *an affecting tale of woe.*

muddle 1. See **confuse. 2.** See **daze.**

muff See **botch.**

multifariousness See **variety.**

multiformity See **variety.**

multiplicity See **variety.**

murky See **dark.**

musing See **pensive.**

mutinous See **rebellious.**

mutiny See **rebellion.**

mutual ***adj.*** **reciprocal, reciprocative.**
Core meaning: Having the same relationship each to the other (*mutual affection*).

nab See **catch.**

nag See **scold.**

naked See **bare.**

name ***n.*** **appellation, denomination, designation, nickname, title.**
NAME is the general term among these related words. A DESIGNATION is a name given to classify or identify: *The correct designation for "heavy hydrogen" is "deuterium."* A DENOMINATION is also a categorizing name; it is applied to persons or things, often religious groups or monetary units, having close relationship: *people of all denominations; bills of small denomination.* A TITLE, applied to persons, indicates rank, office, vocation, etc., and generally connotes distinction; applied to things, such as literary or musical works, it serves to identify. An APPELLATION is a name, other than a proper one, that describes or characterizes and that gains currency more through use than through a formal act of designation: *Abraham Lincoln is known by the appellation "The Great Emancipator."* A NICKNAME is an informal, unofficial, or affectionate name, often a shortened form of a proper name: *Joseph's nickname is Joey.*

nasty See **malevolent.**

nation ***n.*** **commonwealth, country, land, people, race, state.**
NATION primarily signifies a political body—a group of human beings organized under a single government, without close regard for their origins (*the new nations of Africa*); it

also denotes the territory occupied by a political body (*All across the nation new industries are developing*). STATE even more specifically indicates governmental organization, generally on a sovereign basis and in a well-defined area: *the state of Israel.* COMMONWEALTH is used in a political sense to denote the people of a nation or state; it also refers to a nation or state governed by the people: *Australia is a commonwealth.* COUNTRY signifies the territory of one nation (*the country of France*) and is also used in the sense of *nation* (*all the countries of the world*). LAND is a term for a region (*the land of the bison and beaver*); it also can be used to mean *nation* (*the highest elective office in the land*). PEOPLE, in this context, signifies a group united over a long period by common cultural, religious, linguistic, and social ties (*primitive peoples*); it also denotes a body of persons living in the same country under one national government (*the American people*). RACE refers to those recognizable physical traits, stemming from common ancestry, that succeeding generations have in common: *the Caucasian race.*

native ***adj.*** **aboriginal, indigenous.**
NATIVE indicates birth or immediate origin in a specific place: *a native Englishman.* ABORIGINAL describes those who are the first known to have lived in a given region: *aboriginal peoples.* INDIGENOUS specifies that something or someone is of a kind originally living or growing in a region rather than coming or being brought from another part of the world: *The bison is indigenous to North America. The Ainu are indigenous to the northernmost islands of Japan.*
Antonym: **foreign.**

natural ***adj.*** **1. genuine, real.**
NATURAL, GENUINE, and REAL all refer to what is not manmade but is present in or produced by nature: *the moon, a natural satellite of the earth; genuine leather; real sable.*
Antonym: **artificial.**
2. genuine, real, simple, unaffected.
These refer to what shows lack of artifice and affectation. NATURAL stresses spontaneity: *a natural way of speaking.*

GENUINE and REAL suggest that something is free of pretense or falseness: *genuine affection; real humility*. What is SIMPLE is utterly sincere and lacking in deviousness or deceit: *a simple, direct answer*. UNAFFECTED emphasizes lack of affectation: *unaffected behavior*.
Antonym: **affected.**

nature 1. See **disposition. 2.** See **universe.**

nauseate See **repel.**

near ***adj.*** **close, nearby.**
NEAR, CLOSE, and NEARBY refer to what is not far, as in space, time, position, or degree. *Nearby* is the most restricted in application, since it almost always refers to what is located a short distance away: *a nearby city*. *Near* and *close* can be used in this sense, often interchangeably: *The airport is near* (or *close to*) *town*. Both can also imply intimacy of relationship (*near relatives; close friends*).
Antonym: **far.**

nearby See **near.**

nearly See **approximately.**

neat ***adj.*** **orderly, tidy, trim.**
NEAT and its synonyms all describe what is in good or clean condition. *Neat* is the most general: *a neat room; neat handwriting*. ORDERLY implies that which is well arranged or managed and therefore efficient: *an orderly kitchen*. What is TIDY is precisely arranged: *a tidy room; a tidy closet*. TRIM stresses especially pleasing or smart appearance resulting from neatness and tidiness: *looked very trim in his new suit*.
Antonym: **disorderly.**

necessary ***adj.*** **essential, indispensable, vital.**
NECESSARY and its synonyms describe what is needed to achieve a certain result or fulfill a certain requirement. *Necessary* implies that which fills an urgent but not invariably all-compelling need: *fill out the necessary forms*. ESSENTIAL and VITAL refer to what is basic and therefore of crucial importance: *The microscope is an essential tool of science*.

Irrigation was vital to early civilization. INDISPENSABLE even more strongly applies to what cannot be left out or done without: *Oxygen is indispensable for human life.*
Antonym: **unnecessary.**

necessity See **need.**

need *n.* **exigency, necessity, requisite.**
NEED is the most general of these nouns and the least strong in signifying urgency. NECESSITY greatly intensifies urgency; what is a *necessity* is required for the existence, success, or functioning of something: *The sun is a necessity to life on the earth.* EXIGENCY, which is usually plural in this sense, stresses great urgency brought about by particular conditions or circumstances: *the exigencies of war.* REQUISITE specifies need closely associated with the attainment of a given goal: *The first requisite for a successful novel is a good plot.*

needless See **unnecessary.**

negation See **denial.**

neglect *v.* **disregard, shirk, slack.**
Core meaning: To avoid the fulfillment of (*neglected their duty*).

nervous See **upset.**

new *adj.* **fresh, recent.**
NEW applies to what has just been produced or made (*a new movie; a new car*) or has never been used or worn (*a new typewriter; new clothes*). What is FRESH is not yet old; the term suggests unspoiled quality: *fresh eggs.* RECENT stresses the fact that something has been in existence for a short time: *a summary of recent events.* See also **fresh; strange.**
Antonym: **old.**

nickname See **name.**

nimble See **graceful.**

nonappearance See **absence.**

nonattendance See **absence.**

nonchalance See **equanimity.**

nonessential See **unnecessary.**

normal ***adj.*** **regular, standard, typical.**

NORMAL refers to what conforms to or constitutes a usual pattern, level, or category (*his normal weight; normal room temperature*); more specifically it describes what functions in a natural, healthy way (*normal digestion; normal growth*). REGULAR and STANDARD indicate conformity to a pattern in an impersonal sense: *sold radios at 25 per cent off the regular price; a standard sort of horror movie*. TYPICAL stresses the traits or characteristics peculiar to a kind, group, or category: *a typical college professor*.

Antonym: **abnormal.**

nosy See **curious.**

note 1. See **sign. 2.** See **notice.**

notice ***n.*** **attention, cognizance, heed, mark, note, regard.**

Core meaning: The act of observing or taking into account (*took notice of the young executive's drive*).

noticeable See **perceptible.**

novel 1. See **fresh. 2.** See **unconventional.**

novelty ***n.*** **freshness, originality.**

Core meaning: The quality of being new and different (*acclaimed the novelty of his ideas*).

nub See **heart.**

nude See **bare.**

null See **invalid.**

numb See **deaden.**

nuptials See **marriage.**

obedient See **submission.**

obese See **fat.**

obey ***v.*** **comply, follow, mind.**

OBEY and COMPLY both mean to act in accordance with a request, rule, order, or the like. *Obey* suggests the accep-

tance of authority (*obeying traffic regulations*); *comply,* the disposition to yield without protest (*The singer complied with the audience's request by singing an encore*). FOLLOW suggests adherence to a prescribed course of action: *followed the doctor's orders.* MIND applies particularly to children on good behavior: *He minds his mother.*
Antonym: **command.**

objection ***n.*** **challenge, protest, remonstrance.**
Core meaning: The act of expressing strong or reasoned opposition (*a decision made despite the objections of the staff*).

objectionable See **unpleasant.**

obligatory See **compulsory.**

obliging See **amiable.**

obliterate See **abolish.**

obloquy 1. See **dishonor. 2.** See **tirade.**

obscene See **coarse.**

obscure ***adj.*** **unknown.**
These two describe what has not attracted widespread notice: *obscure members of the clergy; unknown legal treatises.* See also **ambiguous.**
Antonym: **famous.**

observant See **alert.**

obstinate ***adj.*** **dogged, headstrong, intractable, intransigent, refractory.**
Core meaning: Tenaciously unwilling to yield (*an obstinate man who never apologized*).

obstruct See **hinder.**

obtuse See **dull.**

occasion See **opportunity.**

occupation See **work.**

odd See **strange.**

odium See **dishonor.**

offbeat See **unconventional.**

offend *v.* **affront, insult, outrage.**

OFFEND is the least emphatic of these verbs, which denote the act of giving displeasure; it often makes no implication regarding intent. To INSULT is to speak to or treat with contempt; it implies a deliberate act calculated to cause humiliation. AFFRONT strengthens this sense of open insult. OUTRAGE, stronger still, emphasizes what causes extreme resentment by flagrant violation of standards of right and decency. See also **displease.**

offer *v.* **present, proffer, tender.**

OFFER is the basic, general term among this group of verbs, which all refer to putting something forward for acceptance or refusal. PROFFER is somewhat more emphatic through its implication of voluntary action motivated by courtesy or generosity: *proffered her help to a blind man at a street corner.* TENDER, in business or legal usage, may stress formality (*tender one's resignation*), or it may apply specifically to discharge of an obligation (*tender payment*); in more general usage it emphasizes formality and observance of amenities (*tender one's respects*). PRESENT stresses formality: *The ambassador presented his credentials to the king.*

offshoot See **branch.**

ogle See **gaze.**

oily See **unctuous.**

old *adj.* **1. aged, elderly, venerable.**

These terms apply to persons. OLD, while the most general, often strongly stresses advanced years: *an old man with a white beard.* ELDERLY specifies the period past late middle age without necessarily implying decline: *an elderly gentleman.* AGED emphasizes advanced years and sometimes suggests infirmity: *an aged couple living in retirement.* VENERABLE implies dignity and qualities associated with age that are worthy of great respect: *a venerable senator.*
Antonym: **young.**

2. used, worn.
OLD applies to what is not of recent make (*a collection of old paperweights*); USED, to what is secondhand (*a used car; used clothing*); and WORN, to what is damaged by wear or use (*worn, faded trousers*).
Antonym: **new.**
3. ancient, antique, archaic, olden.
These all describe what belongs to an earlier time or period. OLD is the general term: *an old Roman bronze*. ANCIENT suggests the remote past (*ancient history*); ARCHAIC refers to primitive times (*an archaic religion*) or to what is not current (*archaic laws*). ANTIQUE is applied both to what is very old and to what has acquired added value through age: *antique furniture*. OLDEN often suggests a note of nostalgia: *in olden days*.
Antonym: **modern.**

olden See **old.**

omen ***n.*** **augury, portent, presage.**
Core meaning: A sign or warning of some future good or evil (*saw omens of trouble to come*).

omnivorous See **voracious.**

open See **spread.**

open-eyed See **alert.**

opening See **opportunity.**

operate ***v.*** **function, go, run, work.**
Core meaning: To act effectively (*The machine doesn't operate half the time*).

opinion ***n.*** **belief, conviction, feeling, judgment, persuasion, sentiment, view.**
An OPINION is any conclusion held with confidence but not supported by positive knowledge or proof: *a man who mistook opinion for fact*. VIEW stresses individuality of outlook as a determinant of the conclusion: *her views on education*. SENTIMENT and especially FEELING are views or attitudes based on emotion rather than reason: *public sentiment*

against foreign wars; his religious feelings. A BELIEF is a conclusion to which one subscribes strongly: *It is my belief that justice will prevail.* CONVICTION is belief that excludes doubt: *my conviction that he is a dishonest person.* PERSUASION applies to a strong belief but does not necessarily suggest an intellectual basis: *of a certain political persuasion.* JUDGMENT, strictly, is opinion based on reasoning and evaluation rather than emotion or will: *In my judgment now is the time to sell.*

opponent ***n.*** **adversary, antagonist, competitor, rival.** All of these nouns refer to persons engaged in contests or struggles. An OPPONENT is a person or group that opposes another, as in a battle, controversy, etc. ADVERSARY suggests a more formidable opponent, while an ANTAGONIST is an actively hostile opponent. COMPETITOR, a milder word, suggests a person trying to outdo one or more opponents, as in sports or business. RIVAL most frequently implies a single, more personal opponent who is competing for the same objective.

opportunity ***n.*** **break, chance, occasion, opening.** OPPORTUNITY and its synonyms refer to a favorable or suitable time or circumstance. An *opportunity* is the right moment to take action toward a certain purpose: *taking the opportunity to go to Europe.* OCCASION, weaker than *opportunity,* suggests the appropriate time for action: *took the occasion to ask her to the celebration.* An OPENING is either an unexpected or an awaited opportunity, as to embark on a new career, launch an enterprise, etc.: *waited for an opening in the conversation to make known his opinion.* CHANCE often implies luck or accident in the arrival of an opportunity: *never had the chance to study photography.* BREAK adds to *chance* the idea that adverse circumstances have unexpectedly become favorable: *had a lucky break and was promoted.*

oppose 1. See **repel. 2.** See **withstand.**

opprobrious See **abusive.**

opprobrium See **dishonor.**

optimistic ***adj.*** **hopeful, rosy, sanguine.**
Core meaning: Expecting a favorable outcome (*optimistic about the future of the company*).

option See **choice.**

optional ***adj.*** **elective, voluntary.**
These three describe what is not required by laws, rules, or regulations. OPTIONAL often suggests that something may be included or not as one wishes: *Whitewall tires and bucket seats are optional.* ELECTIVE implies free choice: *The school offers a wide selection of elective courses.* VOLUNTARY applies to what one does of one's own accord: *voluntary military service.*
Antonym: **compulsory.**

opulent See **luxurious.**

oration See **speech.**

order 1. See **command.** 2. See **union.**

orderly See **neat.**

ordinary 1. See **common.** 2. See **familiar.**

organization See **union.**

origin ***n.*** **inception, root, source.**
ORIGIN and its synonyms relate to beginnings. *Origin,* applicable to persons as well as to things, indicates the often remote time and place when something began: *the origin of life; the origin of a word.* INCEPTION is more specific and marks the actual start of an action or process: *the inception of the space program.* ROOT usually refers to beginning in the sense of fundamental cause or basic reason: *Money is the root of all evil.* SOURCE stresses a place or thing from which something is derived or comes into being (*used the sea as a source of food*); it may also denote a person or printed work considered as a giver of information (*used newspaper articles as the source for his report*).

original See **authentic.**

originality See **novelty.**

ornate See **elaborate.**

orthodox See **conventional.**

outcome See **effect.**

outdo See **surpass.**

outline See **draft.**

outlook 1. See **posture. 2.** See **view.**

output See **production.**

outrage See **offend.**

outrageous ***adj.*** **flagrant, infamous, monstrous.**
These adjectives describe behavior that is grossly offensive or revolting to society; they are often used interchangeably. OUTRAGEOUS applies to what is so distasteful or appalling as to be shocking or intolerable: *an outrageous remark; outrageous prices*. FLAGRANT often adds to *outrageous* the idea of defiance of recognized authority: *a flagrant violation of the law*. INFAMOUS has a personal sense, suggesting bad reputation and notoriety: *an infamous murderer*. MONSTROUS describes actions so outrageous as to be almost inhuman: *Kidnapping is a monstrous act*.

outright See **utter.**

outshine See **surpass.**

outstretch See **spread.**

outstrip See **surpass.**

overbearing See **dictatorial.**

overdue See **late.**

oversight See **error.**

overthrow ***v.*** **overturn, topple, tumble.**
Core meaning: To bring about the downfall of (*rebels trying to overthrow the government*).

overturn See **overthrow.**

own See **acknowledge.**

pacify ***v.*** **appease, assuage, conciliate, mollify, placate, propitiate.**
Core meaning: To ease the anger or agitation of (*managed to pacify the irate customer*).

pain See **distress.**

painstaking See **careful.**

pair See **couple.**

palatial See **luxurious.**

palpable See **perceptible.**

pamper ***v.*** **baby, coddle, humor, indulge, spoil.**
These all refer to catering excessively to another's—or one's own—desires or feelings. INDULGE is applied principally to desires, appetites, and special pleasures, sometimes without very strong condemnation: *indulged my craving for candy.* To PAMPER is to treat with extreme indulgence; it often suggests overattentiveness to physical comforts: *pampered their only child.* HUMOR implies short-term compliance with another's wishes, mood, or idiosyncrasies: *good-naturedly humoring her aunt.* SPOIL usually implies a long-term oversolicitude that badly affects a person's character: *spoiling his son by giving him a big allowance and no responsibilities.* CODDLE points to tender, often overtender care: *coddled his young wife.* BABY suggests bestowing on someone the indulgence and attention appropriate to an infant; it is always unfavorable: *annoyed her grown son by hovering over him and babying him.*

par See **equivalence.**

parallel ***adj.*** **coextensive, collateral, concurrent.**
Core meaning: Lying in the same plane but not intersecting (*parallel roads*).

pardon ***v.*** **excuse, forgive.**
These verbs denote withholding punishment or blame for an offense or fault. To PARDON is to pass over an offense without demanding punishment or subjecting to disfavor: *The queen pardoned a dozen offenders in honor of her birthday.*

FORGIVE implies giving up all resentment as well as all claim to retribution: *forgave him for stealing the family silver.* EXCUSE suggests making allowance for or overlooking an offense: *Excuse me for what I said yesterday.*

Antonym: **punish.**

parity See **equivalence.**

parlance See **wording.**

parley See **deliberation.**

parody See **imitate.**

part See **separate.**

partner ***n.*** **accomplice, ally, associate, colleague, confederate.**

PARTNER and its synonyms all denote one who cooperates in a venture, occupation, or challenge. *Partner* implies a relationship, frequently between two people, in which each has equal status and a certain independence but also has implicit or formal obligation to the other or others. A COLLEAGUE is a fellow member of a profession, staff, or organization. An ALLY is one who, out of a common cause, has taken one's side and can be relied upon, at least temporarily. CONFEDERATE, in this sense, and ACCOMPLICE are both derogatory; they are usually applied to alleged criminals and suggest guilt by willful association. *Confederate* is the more general, signifying any collaborator in a suspicious relationship or venture. An *accomplice* is more specifically somebody who assists a lawbreaker in a crime, without necessarily being present at the time of the crime. An ASSOCIATE is broadly anyone who works in the same place (as distinct from the same field) as another, usually in direct contact with him.

party See **combine.**

pass See **surpass.**

pass away See **die.**

passion ***n.*** **ardor, enthusiasm, fervor, zeal.**

All of these nouns denote strong feeling, either sustained or passing, for or about something or somebody. PASSION is a deep, overwhelming feeling or emotion; when directed toward a person, it usually connotes love as well as sexual desire, although it can also refer to hostile emotions such as anger and hatred (*loathe with passion*). Used lightly, it suggests an avid interest, as in an activity or hobby: *a passion for music*. ARDOR can suggest intense devotion to a cause but commonly connotes a warm, rapturous feeling directed toward persons (*The couple embraced with ardor*). ENTHUSIASM reflects excitement and responsiveness to specific or concrete things: *supported the hockey team with enthusiasm*. FERVOR is a highly intense, sustained emotional state, frequently (like *passion*) with a potential loss of control implied: *He fought with fervor*. ZEAL, which sometimes reflects strong, forceful devotion to a specific cause, expresses a driving attraction to something that grows out of motivation or attitude: *studied philosophy with zeal*.

passive See **submissive.**

paste See **hit.**

pathetic See **moving.**

patient *adj.* **forbearing, resigned.**

All of these refer to what is marked by or shows tolerance of trouble, hardship, delay, etc., over a period of time, usually without complaint though not necessarily without annoyance. PATIENT often implies calm that comes from understanding: *a patient teacher who realizes how difficult it is to learn to read*. FORBEARING suggests restraint, often in the face of considerable provocation: *the forbearing parents of a rebellious teenager*. RESIGNED implies a feeling of failure or of passive acceptance: *resigned to his lot in life*. *Antonym:* **impatient.**

pay See **wage(s).**

peace See **tranquillity.**

peaceful See **calm.**

peak See **climax.**

peculiar 1. See **characteristic. 2.** See **strange.**

peddle See **sell.**

peer See **gaze.**

peeve See **annoy.**

penalize See **punish.**

pendulous See **hanging.**

pensile See **hanging.**

pensive *adj.* **meditative, musing, wistful.**
Core meaning: Suggestive of or expressing deep thoughtfulness (*a pensive mood*).

people See **nation.**

pep See **spirit.**

perceptible *adj.* **appreciable, discernible, noticeable, palpable.**
These describe what can be seen, measured, or detected. PERCEPTIBLE applies to what can be apprehended by the senses or the mind: *a perceptible improvement in the patient's condition.* APPRECIABLE refers to what is considerable in a quantitative sense: *an appreciable amount of atomic waste.* What is DISCERNIBLE can be recognized through scrutiny: *no discernible progress in the negotiations.* NOTICEABLE applies to what is adequately revealed or observable: *a noticeable tremor in his voice.* PALPABLE refers to what can be touched or felt (*a palpable oil*) and to what is easily perceived, even obvious (*a palpable feeling of anger*).
Antonym: **imperceptible.**

perchance See **maybe.**

perfect *adj.* **faultless, flawless, impeccable.**
These describe what has no defects, flaws, errors, etc.; they can be used interchangeably: *a perfect piece of marble; a faultless performance of the sonata; a flawless diamond; impeccable table manners.*
Antonym: **imperfect.**

perhaps See **maybe.**

peril See **danger.**

period See **age.**

periphery See **border.**

perish See **die.**

permanent *adj.* **enduring, eternal, perpetual.**
These all apply to what is lasting or meant to last indefinitely. PERMANENT is the most general. ENDURING usually suggests what is not dimmed or changed by the passage of time: *enduring fame.* ETERNAL and PERPETUAL imply uninterrupted existence unaffected by time: *eternal truths; the perpetual ice and snow of the polar regions.*
Antonym: **temporary.**

permission *n.* **allowance, authorization, consent, license, sanction.**
Core meaning: Approval for an action (*received permission to go ahead with the project*).

permit *v.* **allow, let.**
These are compared in the meaning "to consent to something." Inherent in both PERMIT and ALLOW is the ability to prevent an act. *Permit,* however, suggests authoritative consent (*permit smoking*); *allow*, mere refraining from any hindrance (*Please allow me to finish*). LET often suggests weak consent or failure to prevent something: *His mother let him go to the rock concert even though she disapproved.*
Antonym: **forbid.**

perpendicular See **vertical.**

perpetual See **permanent.**

perpetuate See **immortalize.**

persistent See **chronic.**

personal See **private.**

personality See **disposition.**

perspective See **view.**

persuasion See **opinion.**

pertinent See **relevant.**

perverse See **contrary.**

pet See **caress.**

phenomenal See **fabulous.**

phraseology See **wording.**

phrasing See **wording.**

pick See **choose.**

pictorial See **graphic.**

piece See **cut.**

pinnacle See **climax.**

pious See **holy.**

pith See **heart.**

pithy See **concise.**

pitiless See **cruel.**

placate See **pacify.**

placid See **calm.**

plague See **afflict.**

plain *adj.* **austere, modest, severe, simple.**
PLAIN and its synonyms apply to what is not showy, elaborate, or luxurious. *Plain* and SIMPLE can be used interchangeably in this meaning: *a plain* (or *simple*) *dress; plain* (or *simple*) *food.* AUSTERE and SEVERE imply extreme simplicity, even to the point of total lack of decoration or ornamentation: *austere living quarters; a severe black dress.* MODEST stresses lack of pretension: *a modest summer cottage.*
Antonym: **elaborate.**

plane See **level.**

play See **fiddle.**

plead See **urge.**

pleasant *adj.* **agreeable, gratifying, pleasing, welcome.**
These words describe what gives delight or satisfaction: *a pleasant guest; a pleasant visit; an agreeable hostess; an*

agreeable aroma; a gratifying response to the offer; election results that were gratifying; a pleasing personality; a pleasing furniture arrangement; a welcome visitor; a welcome change.
Antonym: **unpleasant.**

please ***v.*** **delight, gratify.**
To PLEASE is to give enjoyment or satisfaction: *The island pleased the vacationers. The new employee was eager to please.* DELIGHT suggests great pleasure or enjoyment: *I was delighted to run into my old friend after all these years.* GRATIFY especially emphasizes satisfaction, as from deserved recognition, fulfillment of a need, etc.: *His scientific achievements gratified his father.*
Antonym: **displease.**

pleasing See **pleasant.**

pleasure See **joy.**

pledge ***v.*** **1. promise, swear, vow.**
Core meaning: To guarantee by a solemn promise (*pledged financial assistance*).
2. See **devote.**

pliant See **flexible.**

plight See **predicament.**

plot See **conspiracy.**

plug See **advertise.**

plump See **fat.**

plush See **luxurious.**

ply See **handle.**

poignant See **moving.**

poisonous See **malevolent.**

polite ***adj.*** **civil, courteous.**
These apply to proper and mannerly persons and behavior. POLITE is the least specific: *a polite boy; polite applause.* CIVIL suggests reserve, formality, and a minimum of friend-

liness and tact: *Can't you give me a civil answer?* COURTEOUS implies kind and warm graciousness: *a courteous host.* See also **refined.**
Antonym: **impolite.**

polluted See **impure.**

ponderous See **heavy.**

poor *adj.* **destitute, impoverished, indigent.**
All of these refer to persons who have little or no money, wealth, or income. POOR and INDIGENT, the more formal term, can be used interchangeably: *a poor* (or *indigent*) *family who cannot afford to buy groceries.* IMPOVERISHED suggests that someone has been reduced to poverty but may once not have been poor: *impoverished people who had to sell the family silver.* DESTITUTE, the strongest of these words, implies complete poverty: *left destitute after the flood. Poor* and *impoverished* can be used figuratively to describe something that lacks natural richness or strength: *poor* (or *impoverished*) *soil.*
Antonym: **rich.**

popular See **public.**

portent See **omen.**

portion See **cut.**

pose See **affectation.**

position See **posture.**

possess See **carry.**

possessions See **holdings.**

possibility *n.* **contingency, eventuality.**
Core meaning: Something that may occur or be done (*Rain is a real possibility tonight*).

possible *adj.* **feasible, practicable.**
POSSIBLE applies to what can be realized or accomplished: *It may be possible to get there by helicopter.* Something is FEASIBLE if it is clearly possible and likely to be carried out: *a feasible plan for new housing.* PRACTICABLE describes

what is fitted for actual application: *a practicable solution to the problem.*
Antonym: **impossible.**

posterity See **descendant.**

posture ***n.*** **attitude, outlook, position, stance.**
Core meaning: A frame of mind affecting one's thoughts or behavior (*a defeatist posture*).

power ***n.*** **authority, control.**
These nouns denote the right or ability to dominate or rule others. POWER is the most general; it applies whether it is based on rank, position, character, or other advantages: *the absolute power of an emperor; a general with the power to send troops into action.* AUTHORITY suggests legitimate and recognized power: *The mayor had the authority to dismiss the dishonest commissioner.* CONTROL stresses the right to regulate or direct as well as dominate: *the conductor's control over the orchestra.*

powerless ***adj.*** **helpless, impotent.**
POWERLESS and HELPLESS describe what lacks power or authority, as to act or resist: *powerless people at the mercy of their enemies; helpless to combat superior forces.* IMPOTENT in addition suggests weakness and the inability to act: *a ruler impotent to right a wrong.*
Antonym: **powerful.**

practicable See **possible.**

practical ***adj.*** **functional, serviceable, useful.**
PRACTICAL and its synonyms describe what serves or is capable of serving some purpose. *Practical* often refers to what is designed to serve a purpose, without being decorative (*practical low-heeled shoes*); often it stresses efficiency (*a practical machine*). USEFUL stresses the capacity to be used advantageously: *a useful map; a useful reminder.* FUNCTIONAL applies especially to what is designed for a particular purpose: *functional clothing for infants.* SERVICEABLE often suggests durability and sturdiness: *serviceable work boots.*
Antonym: **impractical.**

praise *v.* **acclaim, commend.**

These are words for expressing approval. To PRAISE is to express one's esteem or admiration: *The customers all praised the restaurant highly. Everyone praised her good sense and learning.* ACCLAIM is often—but not always—used literally to indicate actual applause or cheering: *The audience acclaimed the artist's performance of Chopin. The critics are all acclaiming her new novel.* COMMEND implies speaking well of and is usually more formal and official: *The mayor commended the commission for its thorough report.*

Antonym: **blame.**

precariousness See **instability.**

precept See **law.**

precious 1. See **arty. 2.** See **valuable.**

predestination See **fate.**

predicament *n.* **dilemma, plight, quandary.**

A PREDICAMENT is a difficult or embarrassing situation; it often suggests that one has a puzzling or troublesome decision to make and is considering the problem rationally. A PLIGHT is a serious condition or a situation of difficulty or peril, with the appropriate course of action being less clear. DILEMMA more abstractly denotes a problem that requires a person to choose between courses of action that are equally difficult or unpleasant. QUANDARY, somewhat more formal, suggests a complicated condition of uncertainty or doubt.

predispose See **dispose.**

predominant See **dominant.**

prefatory See **preliminary.**

preference See **choice.**

preliminary *adj.* **introductory, prefatory, preparatory.**

Core meaning: Prior to or preparing for the main action or matter (*preliminary remarks*).

premature See **early.**

premeditated See **intentional.**

preparatory See **preliminary.**

preponderant See **dominant.**

preposterous 1. See **absurd. 2.** See **foolish.**

presage See **omen.**

present See **offer.**

present-day See **modern.**

preserve See **defend.**

press See **urge.**

pressure See **force.**

pretend *v.* **dissemble, feign, simulate.**

These all refer to the false assumption of an identity, manner, or skill. PRETEND is mild in force, implying no evil end, but it can suggest an unsuccessful or transparent attempt to fool others: *pretending to be interested in their conversation.* FEIGN implies more strongly the false assumption of some condition, often to evade the responsibilities incurred by being sincere: *She feigned illness and left early.* DISSEMBLE suggests artful deception in speech or manner to conceal one's true purposes or feelings: *dissembled his disappointment with a show of gaiety.* To SIMULATE is to make a pretense of (*simulated lack of interest*); in another sense the term refers to imitation that closely resembles reality (*a device that simulates space flight*).

pretentious See **arty.**

pretty See **beautiful.**

prevalent See **common.**

priceless See **valuable.**

prime See **excellent.**

principle See **law.**

private *adj.* **personal.**

PRIVATE and PERSONAL both apply to what pertains to or is confined to one particular person: *my private opinion; a*

personal experience. Both can suggest what is intimate or even secret: *a private thought; a personal letter. Private* also refers to what is not available for public use or participation (*a private club; a private party*) and to what is owned by a person or group rather than the public or government (*a private house; private property*).
Antonym: **public.**

prize See **appreciate.**

probable See **likely.**

procedure See **move.**

proceed See **advance.**

produce See **create.**

product See **production.**

production ***n.*** **output, product, yield.**
Core meaning: The amount or quantity produced (*keeping production up to meet the demand*).

professional ***n.*** **authority, expert, master.**
A PROFESSIONAL is someone who follows or makes a living at an occupation requiring training and specialized study: *The actors in this troupe are all professionals*. An AUTHORITY is someone who is an accepted source of expert information: *an authority on medieval history*. An EXPERT is a person with great knowledge, skill, and experience in a given field: *a leading foreign-policy expert*. A MASTER is someone who has gained complete command of a skill or craft: *a master in cabinetmaking*.
Antonym: **amateur.**

proffer See **offer.**

proficiency See **expertise.**

profligate See **immoral.**

profound See **deep.**

progenitor See **ancestor.**

progeny See **descendant.**

program *n.* **agenda, calendar, docket, schedule.**
Core meaning: An organized list of activities, events, etc. (*A visit to the factory is on today's program*).

progress See **advance.**

prohibit See **forbid.**

prolific See **fertile.**

prolixity See **wordiness.**

prolonged See **chronic.**

promise See **pledge.**

promote *v.* **1. cultivate, encourage, foster.**
Core meaning: To help bring about (*Does TV promote violence?*).
2. See **advance.**
3. See **advertise.**

promulgate See **advertise.**

proper See **suitable.**

property See **holding(s).**

propitiate See **pacify.**

propitious See **favorable.**

prospect See **view.**

prosper See **succeed.**

protect See **defend.**

protest See **objection.**

protracted See **chronic.**

proud *adj.* **arrogant, disdainful, haughty, supercilious.**
These words imply self-esteem, most of them to the degree of belief in one's superiority over others. PROUD applies to persons who feel justifiable satisfaction over something they own, make, do, or are a part of (*proud to be named to the Olympic team; proud to be an American*); it sometimes suggests conceit or arrogance (*too proud to talk to those who had less education*). ARROGANT refers to those who

assume excessive and unpleasant self-importance: *the arrogant manners of the maître d'*. DISDAINFUL suggests scorn and contempt: *a cold, disdainful stare*. HAUGHTY refers to an attitude of superiority, often because of one's birth or station: *a haughty aristocrat*. SUPERCILIOUS combines the meanings of *haughty* and *disdainful: a supercilious smile*.
***Antonym:* humble.**

prove *v.* **demonstrate, establish.**
These verbs share the sense of establishing that something is true or valid by presenting evidence or arguments: *proved the charge of murder at the trial; demonstrate* (or *establish*) *one's innocence of an accusation*. They can also be used to mean "show convincingly": *proved he could lift 400 pounds; demonstrated his ability to do the job; establishing that the earth moves around the sun*.
***Antonym:* disprove.**

provident See **economical.**

provisional 1. See **temporary. 2.** See **conditional.**

provisory See **conditional.**

provoke *v.* **1. arouse, excite, goad, impel, incite, inflame, kindle, motivate, move, rouse, spur, stimulate.**
Core meaning: To stir to action or feeling (*carelessness that provoked anger*).
2. See **annoy.**

prudence *n.* **circumspection, discretion.**
These nouns are compared as they express caution and wisdom. PRUDENCE, the most comprehensive, implies not only caution but also the capacity to judge in advance the probable results of one's actions. DISCRETION suggests prudence coupled with self-restraint and sound judgment. CIRCUMSPECTION adds to *discretion* the implication of wariness in one's actions out of heedfulness for circumstances or consequences.

prudent 1. See **careful. 2.** See **economical. 3.** See **wise.**

psyche See **psychology.**

psychology ***n.*** **ethos, mentality, mind, psyche.**
Core meaning: The thought processes characteristic of an individual or group (*the psychology of today's youth*).

public ***adj.*** **general, popular.**
These adjectives describe what pertains to, affects, or represents the people at large: *public opinion; public safety; the general welfare; the popular vote. Public* also applies to what is supported by, used by, or open to the people or community: *the public library; a public telephone. General* and *popular* refer to what is widespread or prevalent: *general discontent; a popular idea.*
Antonym: **private.**

punish ***v.*** **chastise, discipline, penalize.**
These verbs refer to different ways of causing someone to undergo a penalty for a crime, fault, or misbehavior. PUNISH applies whether the penalty takes the form of money, time in jail, or physical pain. CHASTISE often refers specifically to physical punishment, but it also means to criticize severely. DISCIPLINE stresses punishment designed to control an offender and to eliminate unacceptable conduct: *discipline an unruly child.* PENALIZE is the weakest of these terms; it usually involves the forfeit of money or privileges for breaking a code of fair play or established conduct.
Antonym: **pardon.**

purchase See **buy.**

pure See **moral.**

purview See **ken.**

push 1. See **sell. 2.** See **advertise. 3.** See **ambition.**

quack See **impostor.**

quaint See **strange.**

quake See **shake.**

qualification ***n.*** **eligibility, fitness, suitableness.**
Core meaning: The quality or state of being eligible (*had all the qualifications for the job*).

qualified See **able.**

qualm *n.* **compunction, misgiving, reservation, scruple.** QUALM and its synonyms denote varying degrees of uncertainty felt by a person about his or her judgment in taking action. *Qualm* can be as slight as a feeling of uneasiness or as strong as a queasy sensation in its implication of self-doubt. SCRUPLE is hesitation—or a feeling producing hesitation—based on one's conscience. COMPUNCTION stresses the importance of conscience in deciding the rightness or wrongness of one's acts; it often refers to a feeling that one has done something one ought not to have done. MISGIVING implies doubt or concern as to one's ability or fear that one has made a mistake. RESERVATION also connotes doubt about the fitness or correctness of an action; it refers to a rather well-defined limiting condition that one has arrived at (*has reservations about the proposal*).

quandary See **predicament.**

quarrel See **argue.**

queer See **strange.**

quench See **extinguish.**

quick See **fast.**

quick-witted See **shrewd.**

quiet *adj.* **restrained, subdued, unobtrusive.** *Core meaning:* Not showy or obtrusive (*a room decorated in a quiet, pleasing style*).

quip See **joke.**

quirk See **eccentricity.**

quiver See **shake.**

quixotic See **idealistic.**

race See **nation.**

rack See **afflict.**

radical *adj.* **basic, fundamental, underlying.** *Core meaning:* Arising from or going to the root or source (*radical differences about the very purpose of the organization*).

rage See **anger.**

rail See **scold.**

raise ***v.*** **boost, heave, hoist, lift.**
These verbs mean to move or bring something from a lower level to a higher one, often in a figurative sense. RAISE implies movement to a higher position (*raise the window slightly; raise a drawbridge*); figuratively it suggests movement to a higher plane or level (*raise the tone of a discussion*). LIFT stresses the effort involved: *a suitcase that is too heavy to lift.* HOIST is applied chiefly to the lifting of heavy objects, often by mechanical means (*hoist a sunken ship*), and HEAVE, to lifting or raising that requires great exertion (*heaved the pack onto his back*). BOOST refers to upward movement effected by pushing from below (*boosted her into the saddle*); figuratively it applies to an increase or advance in amount, degree, status, etc.: *boost sales; boost morale.*
Antonym: **lower.**

random See **accidental.**

range See **ken.**

rank See **flagrant.**

rapacious See **voracious.**

rapid See **fast.**

rare See **uncommon.**

rate See **earn.**

ratiocination See **logic.**

rationale See **explanation.**

rationality See **logic.**

rationalization See **explanation.**

ravenous See **voracious.**

raze See **destroy.**

reach 1. ***v.*** **accomplish, achieve, attain, gain.**
These verbs refer to the attainment of certain objectives. REACH connotes arriving at a goal through effort or progress: *jets reaching supersonic speeds; reaching old age.* ACCOMPLISH implies successful completion: *accomplish an assignment.* ACHIEVE suggests the successful accomplishment of something important, as through skill or initiative: *achieved the desired effect; achieve recognition.* ATTAIN may imply great effort: *Correct grammar is a tool for attaining confidence in writing and speaking.* GAIN connotes arriving at a goal despite considerable effort in surmounting obstacles: *The troops gained the hill.*
2. ***n.*** See **ken.**

reactionary ***adj.*** **backward, unprogressive.**
Core meaning: Clinging to obsolete ideas (*reactionary views on civil rights*).

real 1. See **natural. 2.** See **authentic.**

realistic See **graphic.**

really See **actually.**

reason See **logic.**

reasonable See **sensible.**

rebellion ***n.*** **insurrection, mutiny, revolt, revolution, riot, uprising.**
These terms pertain in varying degree to opposition to existing order or authority. REBELLION is defiance of authority in general or open but unorganized disobedience (*teen-age rebellion*); it is also open, armed, and organized opposition to constituted political authority that often fails in its purpose (*Shays' Rebellion*). A REVOLUTION is a radical alteration in a system or in social conditions (*the industrial revolution*); it is also the overthrow by open, organized armed force of a government and its replacement with another (*the American Revolution*). REVOLT is widespread opposition to prevailing standards (*a taxpayers' revolt*); like INSURRECTION and UPRISING, it is also an armed attempt to change authority. A RIOT is a sudden, violent, disorganized uprising, fre-

quently unarmed and unplanned. MUTINY is open rebellion against constituted authority, especially by subordinates in the armed forces.

rebellious ***adj.*** **insubordinate, mutinous.**
These apply to what resists authority. REBELLIOUS is the least specific: *a rebellious child; a rebellious prisoner.* INSUBORDINATE specifically implies the refusal or failure to recognize the authority of a superior: *The general demoted his aide for his insubordinate behavior.* MUTINOUS pertains to rising up against lawful authority, especially that of a naval or military command: *The mutinous seamen were sent to walk the plank.*
Antonym: **submissive.**

rebuff See **reject.**

rebuke See **admonish.**

rebut See **disprove.**

recall See **remember.**

recede ***v.*** **regress, retire, retreat, withdraw.**
These verbs describe motion backward, literally or figuratively. RECEDE suggests motion backward from a limit, point, or mark: *a hairline that is receding; a tide that receded, exposing barnacle-covered rocks.* REGRESS suggests a return to an earlier condition, often even the reversal or undoing of progress: *Under hypnosis he regressed to childhood.* RETIRE implies moving back either in space or from a social environment: *He retired to his study. He retired early from his career.* WITHDRAW denotes moving back but also applies to getting out of a commitment or obligation: *He withdrew from the campaign.* RETREAT suggests withdrawal, often to avoid danger or attack: *The troops retreated rapidly.*
Antonym: **advance.**

receive See **accept.**

recent See **new.**

reciprocal See **mutual.**

reciprocative See **mutual.**

reclaim See **save.**

recollect See **remember.**

reconcile *v.* **reunite.**

These refer to the restoration of harmonious relations after a period of anger or discontent. RECONCILE focuses on the renewed state of peace or affection: *The politicians reconciled after the election. After they realized what fools they had been, the lovers were quickly reconciled.* REUNITE often suggests no more than coming together after a separation (*The friends were reunited years after the shipwreck*), but as a synonym of *reconcile* it suggests the mending of a split: *Three years after their divorce his parents were reunited.*
Antonym: **estrange.**

recondite See ambiguous.

recoup See **recover.**

recover *v.* **recoup, regain, retrieve.**

To RECOVER is to get back something lost: *a crusade to recover the Holy Land.* REGAIN suggests efforts to get back something lost or taken from one, usually a quality or status rather than an object: *regaining his health; regained her freedom.* RECOUP means getting back the equivalent of something lost or damaged: *losses that can never be recouped.* RETRIEVE emphasizes effort and very often pertains to the physical recovery of a thing (*retrieved the ball in the end zone*); it can also refer to making good or putting right what is bad, wrong, etc. (*retrieving an error*). See also **find.**

recreation *n.* **amusement, diversion, entertainment.**

These nouns refer to activity that refreshes the mind or body after work. RECREATION implies something that restores one's strength, spirits, or vitality: *played tennis for recreation.* AMUSEMENT suggests that which occupies in an agreeable or pleasing fashion: *performed music for their own amusement.* DIVERSION suggests something to take one's attention off customary affairs: *went shopping for diversion.* ENTERTAINMENT shares these meanings but especially suggests a performance or show that is designed to amuse or divert.

rectify See **correct.**

recur See **return.**

redeem See **save.**

redress See **correct.**

reduce 1. See **decrease. 2.** See **lower.**

reduction See **depreciation.**

referee See **judge.**

refined ***adj.*** **cultivated, cultured, genteel, polite.**
As it describes a material property REFINED means "free of impurities." It has a figurative meaning that describes freedom from coarseness or vulgarity (*a refined young woman*); its synonyms share this meaning. CULTIVATED and CULTURED both imply refinement, good manners, and the appreciation of what is beautiful and civilized: *a cultivated person; a cultured gentleman who collects paintings.* GENTEEL describes a person who is both well-bred and polite: *a poor but genteel family.* POLITE stresses good manners, tact, and consideration for others: *a polite child; a polite letter.*
Antonym: **coarse.**

reform See **correct.**

refractory See **obstinate.**

refrain ***v.*** **abstain, forbear, withhold.**
Core meaning: To hold oneself back (*Please refrain from applauding*).

refurbish See **modernize.**

refuse See **reject.**

refute 1. See **deny. 2.** See **disprove.**

regain See **recover.**

regard 1. See **consider. 2.** See **favor. 3.** See **notice.**

region See **area.**

regress See **recede.**

regret 1. See **sorrow. 2.** See **disappointment.**

regular See **normal.**

reiteration See **repetition.**

reject *v.* **decline, rebuff, refuse, spurn.**
These all refer to turning down what is available or offered. REJECT, DECLINE, and REFUSE are the most neutral of the group: *rejected his request for an extension on the loan; declined her invitation; refuse permission to leave early.* REBUFF suggests a blunt or abrupt refusal (*rebuffing his advances*); SPURN, a disdainful or scornful one (*spurn a suitor*). See also **disbelieve.**
Antonym: **accept.**

rejection See **denial.**

rejuvenate See **modernize.**

release See **free.**

relent *v.* **ease off, slacken, soften, weaken, yield.**
Core meaning: To moderate or change a position or course of action (*would not relent despite public opinion*).

relevant *adj.* **germane, material, pertinent.**
RELEVANT and its synonyms describe what is associated with a matter or situation at hand and has direct bearing on it: *Stick to relevant questions, please!* PERTINENT implies a logical and precise bearing: *The pertinent statistics do not confirm the press accounts of the accident.* GERMANE applies to what is so closely akin to the subject as to reinforce it: *statements germane to the topic of his speech.* MATERIAL has the sense of being needed to complete a subject: *material evidence.*
Antonym: **irrelevant.**

reliable *adj.* **dependable, trustworthy.**
RELIABLE implies complete confidence in the honesty or truthfulness of a person (*a reliable witness*) or in the ability

of a person or thing to perform ably (*a reliable doctor; a reliable stove*). DEPENDABLE suggests confidence in the support or strength of a person or thing (*a dependable friend; a dependable elevator*). TRUSTWORTHY applies less often to things; it usually refers to a person who has established his or her right to be considered worthy of another's confidence: *a trustworthy husband.*
Antonym: **unreliable.**

reliance See **confidence.**

religious See **holy.**

relish See **like.**

remedy See **correct.**

remember *v.* **recall, recollect.**
REMEMBER and its synonyms mean to bring back to memory or think of again: *She remembered all the old songs of her childhood. I can never recall names. Do you recollect her address?* More specifically, to *remember* is often to keep something in mind: *Remember to phone your parents! Recall* and *recollect* frequently suggest a deliberate effort to bring something back to mind: *The boy could not recall the circumstances of the accident. It took her a few moments to recollect why she had refused the job offer.*
Antonym: **forget.**

remission See **abeyance.**

remonstrance See **objection.**

remote See **far.**

renowned See **famous.**

rent See **breach.**

repel *v.* **1. combat, fight, oppose, resist.**
These all share the meaning "to struggle against": *repel an invasion; combat an enemy; combat crime; fight an opponent; fight illness; oppose corruption; resist an attack; resist change.*

2. disgust, nauseate, revolt, sicken.
All of these mean "to cause aversion in," whether the strong dislike is physical or emotional: *The shrillness of the voice repelled her. His behavior disgusted his friends. His opinions nauseated his colleagues. His taking advantage of the handicapped revolted everyone who knew about it. The dictator's cruelty sickened liberal citizens.*
Antonym: **attract.**

repetition ***n.*** **iteration, reiteration, restatement.**
Core meaning: The act or process of repeating (*a repetition of past mistakes*).

replete See **full.**

reply See **answer.**

representative ***n.*** **delegate, deputy.**
Core meaning: One who stands or acts for another (*representatives at a convention*).

repress See **forget.**

reprimand See **admonish.**

reproach See **admonish.**

reprove See **admonish.**

requisite See **need.**

rescue See **save.**

resentment See **anger.**

reservation See **qualm.**

reserve See **book.**

resigned See **patient.**

resist 1. See **repel. 2.** See **withstand.**

resolution 1. See **analysis. 2.** See **will.**

resolve 1. See **decide. 2.** See **will.**

respond See **answer.**

responsible See **liable.**

restatement See **repetition.**

restive See **impatient.**

restore See **modernize.**

restrained See **quiet.**

restrict See **limit.**

result See **effect.**

resultant See **effect.**

retail See **sell.**

retard See **delay.**

retire See **recede.**

retort See **answer.**

retreat 1. See **recede. 2.** See **back.**

retrieve See **recover.**

retrograde See **back.**

retrogress See **back.**

return *v.* **recur, revert.**

RETURN, the least specific of these terms, denotes going or coming back to a former place, position, condition, etc. RECUR applies to repeated occurrences of the same thing: *an area where earthquakes recur.* REVERT refers to returning to an earlier and sometimes less desirable condition, belief, interest, etc.: *a neglected garden reverting to a weedy wilderness.*

reunite See **reconcile.**

reveal See **show.**

revelry See **gaiety.**

revengeful See **vindictive.**

reverence See **honor.**

reverse *v.* **invert, transpose.**

REVERSE implies a complete turning about to a contrary position with reference to action, direction, or policy. To INVERT is basically to turn something upside down (*invert a jar*), but it may imply placing something in a contrary order (*invert a sentence by placing the predicate first*). TRANSPOSE applies to altering position in a sequence by reversing or changing the order: *transpose the letters of a word.*

revert See **return.**

review *n.* **1. commentary, criticism, critique.**
Core meaning: Evaluative and critical discourse (*The new book received rave reviews*).
2. See **analysis.**

revile See **scold.**

reviling See **abusive.**

revise See **correct.**

revolt 1. See **rebellion. 2.** See **repel.**

revolting See **unspeakable.**

revolution See **rebellion.**

reward See **bonus.**

rich *adj.* **affluent, wealthy.**
All of these refer to persons who have a great deal of money or income. RICH is the most general and straightforward word (*a rich family*); it can also be used figuratively to describe something that is abundant in natural resources (*rich land*). A WEALTHY person is often a person of substance in a community: *a wealthy patron of the arts.* AFFLUENT sometimes connotes continually increasing prosperity: *an affluent landowner.*
Antonym: **poor.**

ridicule *v.* **deride, gibe, mock, taunt, twit.**
These verbs concern the efforts of one person to find amusement or delight at the expense of another; they vary from mere mischief to sheer malice. RIDICULE refers to the attempt to arouse laughter or merriment at another's expense by making fun of or belittling him. To MOCK is to make fun of a person, often by imitating him or depicting him in an insulting way. TAUNT suggests insult with contempt. DERIDE implies both scorn and contempt in demeaning a person. To TWIT is to tease, especially by calling attention

to something embarrassing. To GIBE is to make heckling or jeering remarks.

ridiculous See **absurd.**

rift See **breach.**

right See **true.**

righteousness See **virtue.**

rigid See **inflexible.**

rigor See **severity.**

rile See **annoy.**

rim See **border.**

ring See **surround.**

riot See **rebellion.**

rise *v.* **ascend, climb, mount, soar.**

These verbs denote a moving upward, but they differ widely in both their literal and their figurative meanings. RISE is applied to a great range of events, chiefly involving steady or customary upward movement: *The sun rises over the eastern horizon. Prices rise and fall.* ASCEND connotes rising step by step, literally or figuratively: *ascend a staircase; ascend through the ranks.* CLIMB suggests steady progress against gravity or some other resistance: *The rocket climbed rapidly. The actress eventually climbed to the top of her profession.* MOUNT often implies reaching a level or limit: *a death toll that mounted; mounting to the top of the hill.* SOAR suggests the effortless attainment of great height (*eagles soaring in the sky*); often it refers to what rises rapidly and suddenly, especially above what is normal (*The cost of living soared*).

Antonym: **fall.**

risible See **laughable.**

risk See **danger.**

ritual *n.* **ceremony, form, formality.**

Core meaning: A formal act or set of acts prescribed by convention or tradition (*the rituals of a religious service*).

rival See **opponent.**

romantic See **idealistic.**

root 1. See **origin. 2.** See **heart.**

rosy See **optimistic.**

rough 1. See **harsh. 2.** See **draft.**

roughly See **approximately.**

roundabout See **indirect.**

rouse See **provoke.**

rout See **defeat.**

rude See **impolite.**

rule 1. See **decide. 2.** See **law.**

run 1. See **administer. 2.** See **operate.**

rupture See **breach.**

sabotage *v.* **subvert, undermine.**

Core meaning: To damage, destroy, or defeat by underhand means (*tried to sabotage the contract negotiations*).

sad *adj.* **blue, dejected, depressed, desolate, melancholy, miserable, sorrowful, unhappy, wretched.**

All of these describe what shows, causes, feels, or expresses low spirits, gloom, etc. SAD and UNHAPPY are the most general: *a sad* (or *unhappy*) *smile; a sad message; an unhappy household.* BLUE implies gloom or depression: *He felt blue when he lost his job.* DEJECTED suggests a dark mood of rather short duration: *He was dejected when she turned him down but quickly found comfort in another.* DEPRESSED and MELANCHOLY refer to lingering periods of somber thoughts: *depressed for several days by the bad news; a melancholy disposition.* DESOLATE implies sadness due to loss or loneliness: *a desolate child whose mother had died.* MISERABLE and WRETCHED refer to any state of profound unhappiness: *made her life miserable; felt wretched when she finally left.* SORROWFUL describes extreme sadness: *a sorrowful voice.*

Antonym: **glad.**

sadistic See **cruel.**

safeguard See **defend.**

safety ***n.*** **security.**

Both SAFETY and SECURITY denote freedom from danger, accident, injury, or the threat of harm: *worked in safety while he was wearing his helmet; lived in the security of his home.*

Antonym: **danger.**

sagacious See **shrewd.**

sage See **wise.**

salary See **wage(s).**

sally See **joke.**

same ***adj.*** **equal, equivalent, identical.**

All of these adjectives refer to the absence of difference or disparity. SAME and IDENTICAL mean the very one, not another: *the same restaurant I went to yesterday; the identical words the President used.* They also apply to things that are exactly alike, as in kind, quality, amount, value, etc., but here *identical* is stronger in specifying strict agreement in every respect and detail: *books of the same size; identical machine parts.* EQUAL refers more generally to absence of difference between two or more things, as in extent, amount, value, etc.: *equal portions; equal rights for women.* What is EQUIVALENT to something else may not be identical but has the same worth, effect, force, or meaning: *francs equivalent to ten American dollars.*

Antonym: **different.**

sanction 1. See **approve. 2.** See **permission.**

sanguine See **optimistic.**

sarcastic ***adj.*** **caustic, ironic, sardonic, satirical.**

SARCASTIC and its synonyms apply to personal expression that is bitter, cutting, or derisive. *Sarcastic* suggests sharp and bitter mockery and ridicule. IRONIC implies a milder and subtler form of mockery; what is *ironic* suggests something different from what is expressed: *an ironic smile.* CAUSTIC can apply to any expression that is biting or cutting. SATIRICAL refers to expression that seeks to expose hypocrisy or foolishness to ridicule, often by using humor or irony. SARDONIC is associated with scorn, derision, mockery, and cynicism.

sardonic See **sarcastic.**

satirical See **sarcastic.**

satisfactory See **sufficient.**

save *v.* **1. deliver, reclaim, redeem, rescue.**
In this sense all these verbs refer to the freeing of a person or thing from danger, evil, confinement, or servitude. SAVE, the most general, applies to any act of preserving from the consequences of danger or evil: *saved her from drowning; saving sinners.* DELIVER applies chiefly to freeing persons from confinement, restraint, or evil: *Deliver us from our enemies.* RECLAIM, when applied to persons, usually means to restore to an earlier state of moral and physical soundness or to reform after a lapse (*reclaimed him from his wicked life*); it can also mean to return or convert a thing to usefulness or productivity (*reclaim eroded soil*). To REDEEM is to free from captivity, pawn, or the consequences of sin, error, or misuse, in every case by the expenditure of money or effort (*redeemed hostages; redeemed his ring from the pawnbroker*). RESCUE usually implies saving from immediate harm or danger by direct action: *rescuing the victim of the fire.*
2. conserve, hoard, husband.
These all refer to the careful use of money, time, energy, or any kind of supply. SAVE can apply to the prevention or reduction of loss, expenditure, or waste (*save money at a sale; save time*) or to the accumulation of something needed for future use (*saved five dollars a week; saving on a monthly basis*). CONSERVE is a more formal term; it usually refers to the protection of something from loss or depletion (*conserved his energy for the last push to win the race*) and often to the taking of systematic measures to keep something in good condition (*Science and common sense tell us we should conserve our forests*). To HUSBAND is to spend or use economically or with care: *husbanded her strength;*

husbanding our resources. HOARD nearly always suggests secretiveness or greed: *hoarded food during a shortage; a miser hoarding gold.*
Antonym: **waste.**

savor See **flavor.**

say ***v.*** **articulate, communicate, convey, express, state, tell, utter, vent, voice.**
Core meaning: To put into words (*said what was on her mind and left*).

scare See **frighten.**

scatter ***v.*** **dispel, disperse, dissipate.**
These all denote separating and going in different directions. SCATTER refers to haphazard and often widespread distribution: *At the bell the class scattered into the hallways. The wind scattered the leaves.* DISPEL usually suggests scattering in a figurative sense: *dispel doubts and fears.* DISPERSE implies the breaking up of a mass or group: *The crowd dispersed at the command of the police.* DISSIPATE suggests a reduction to nothing: *A strong wind dissipated the clouds. His anger soon dissipated.*
Antonym: **gather.**

schedule See **program.**

schism See **breach.**

scholarship See **knowledge.**

scold ***v.*** **berate, nag, rail, revile, upbraid.**
All of these verbs express criticism or disfavor. SCOLD implies anger or irritation and often the tone and manner of one correcting a child at fault. UPBRAID is stronger and generally suggests rather formal criticism, such as that made by a superior. To BERATE is to scold severely and often at length. REVILE especially stresses the use of abusive language. NAG refers to complaining and faultfinding, usually prolonged and persistent. RAIL suggests persistent complaint but also implies bitterness and the use of strong or emphatic language.

scope See **ken.**

scorching See **hot.**

scorn See **despise.**

scourge See **afflict.**

scrumptious See **delicious.**

scruple See **qualm.**

scuffle See **conflict.**

scurrilous See **abusive.**

secluded ***adj.*** **cloistered, isolated, sequestered.**
Core meaning: Solitary and shut off from human contact (*led a secluded life in a convent*).

seclusion See **solitude.**

second See **moment.**

secondary 1. See **subordinate. 2.** See **minor.**

secret ***adj.*** **clandestine, covert, furtive, stealthy, surreptitious, underhand.**
SECRET and its synonyms apply to what is purposely concealed from view or knowledge. *Secret* is the most general and therefore weakest in suggesting anything beyond this basic sense. STEALTHY is most often applied to quiet action designed to avoid attracting notice. COVERT describes any act not taken openly. CLANDESTINE usually implies secrecy for the purpose of concealing some unlawful or improper purpose. FURTIVE suggests the slyness, shiftiness, and evasiveness of a thief. SURREPTITIOUS includes the meanings of *stealthy* and *furtive: a surreptitious glance at his watch.* UNDERHAND implies unfairness, deceit, fraud, or slyness as well as secrecy.

secrete See **hide.**

security See **safety.**

seduce ***v.*** **allure, entice, inveigle, lure, tempt.**
Core meaning: To draw into a wrong or foolish course of action (*seduced into gambling by the vision of easy money*).

see See **foresee.**

seem See **appear.**

seize See **catch.**

select See **choose.**

selection See **choice.**

self-centered See **selfish.**

self-confidence See **confidence.**

selfish ***adj.*** **egotistic, self-centered.**

SELFISH and SELF-CENTERED refer to persons who are concerned chiefly or only with themselves, without regard for the well-being of others. EGOTISTIC (or *egotistical*) implies an exaggerated sense of self-importance.
Antonym: **unselfish.**

selfless See **unselfish.**

sell ***v.*** **market, merchandise, peddle, push, retail, vend.**

These share the meaning of exchanging goods or services for money or its equivalent. However, only SELL and VEND, the more formal of the two, can be used interchangeably: *sells apples; vends caviar.* MARKET means both "to sell" and "to offer for sale": *markets cosmetics; marketing his new invention.* MERCHANDISE has the meanings "buy and sell" and "try to sell," the second meaning shared by one sense of PUSH (the slang sense implies illegal trafficking in narcotics: *pushes heroin*). PEDDLE suggests that the seller travels about rather than keeping a shop: *peddled his wares from a pushcart.* RETAIL specifically entails sale to consumers at full price: *retails blouses and skirts.*
Antonym: **buy.**

send ***v.*** **address, dispatch, transmit.**

These words mean "to cause to be conveyed from one place to another." SEND applies generally: *sent supplies by airlift; send a message; send a shipment.* ADDRESS in this sense implies directing something to a particular place or person: *address a letter.* To DISPATCH is to send to a specific

destination or on specific business: *The commander dispatched six battleships to the scene of the invasion.* TRANSMIT is used especially for signals and messages that travel by television or radio waves: *The astronauts transmitted reports from the moon.*
Antonym: **receive.**

sense See **meaning.**

sensible ***adj.*** **logical, reasonable.**
SENSIBLE and its synonyms describe what is in agreement with common sense. *Sensible* stresses good judgment (*a sensible hat for the occasion*); it shares the implications of REASONABLE, which suggests the ability to think, understand, and make decisions clearly and rationally (*a sensible*—or *reasonable—woman*). LOGICAL emphasizes correct and orderly thought: *a logical reason for going.*
Antonym: **absurd.**

sentiment See **opinion.**

separate ***v.*** **divide, part, sever.**
These verbs refer to setting or keeping apart. SEPARATE applies both to removing a portion or segment from a whole and to keeping apart by occupying a position between things: *He separated the wheat from the chaff. The Pyrenees separate France and Spain.* DIVIDE also has both of these senses. With respect to putting apart, it often implies separation into predetermined portions or groups: *divide a cake.* With respect to keeping apart, *divide* often implies separation into opposing or hostile groups: *Bad feelings have divided the team.* PART refers most often to separation of persons or of segments: *The travelers parted to go their separate ways. The curtains parted.* SEVER usually applies to cutting a part from a whole or cutting a whole into sections; figuratively it applies to ending a relationship: *The woodsman severed a limb from the tree. Diplomatic ties were severed at midnight.* See also **single.**
Antonym: **join.**

sequestered See **secluded.**

serene See **calm.**

serenity 1. See **equanimity. 2.** See **tranquillity.**

serious See **critical.**

serviceable See **practical.**

servitude See **bondage.**

set See **circle.**

settle See **decide.**

sever See **separate.**

severe 1. See **harsh. 2.** See **plain.**

severity ***n.*** **austerity, harshness, rigor, stringency.** *Core meaning:* The fact or condition of being rigorous and unsparing (*an ordeal of extraordinary severity*).

shade See **trace.**

shadowy See **dark.**

shady See **dark.**

shake ***v.*** **quake, quiver, shiver, shudder, tremble, wobble.** SHAKE, the most general of these terms, applies to any involuntary vibrating movement in a thing or a person: *The earthquake shook the ground. Jack shook with anger.* TREMBLE implies quick and rather slight movement, like that of a person affected by anger, cold, etc.: *leaves trembling in the breeze; a woman trembling with fear.* QUAKE refers to shaking or vibrating movement such as that caused by physical or emotional upheaval: *The ground quaked as the stampede passed. He had such stage fright that his legs quaked under him.* QUIVER suggests a slight and tremulous movement: *lips quivering with excitement.* SHIVER involves rapid and rather slight movement: *shivering in the cold.* SHUDDER chiefly applies to sudden strong, convulsive shaking, as that caused by fear, horror, or a revolting sight or thought. WOBBLE refers to pronounced and unsteady movement: *wobbled the table when he sat down; an old table that wobbles.*

shakiness See **instability.**

shallow ***adj.*** **superficial.**
SHALLOW literally describes what has little physical depth (*a shallow lake*); SUPERFICIAL, what pertains to a surface (*a superficial cut*). Figuratively *shallow* refers to what lacks depth of thought or feeling: *shallow ideas. Superficial* implies a concern only with what is apparent or obvious: *a superficial interest.*
Antonym: **deep.**

shame See **dishonor.**

shameless See **bold.**

shape See **make.**

sharp ***adj.*** **acute, keen.**
These adjectives describe edges or points that are not dull. SHARP applies to what can easily pierce or cut: *a sharp razor; a sharp knife.* KEEN usually specifies a long, sharp cutting edge: *a keen sword.* ACUTE applies to what has a pointed tip or end: *an acute mountain peak.* Figuratively *sharp* suggests cleverness (*a sharp mind*); *keen* implies astuteness and discernment (*a keen observer of men*); and *acute* even more strongly implies perceptiveness (*an acute awareness of one's surroundings*).
Antonym: **dull.**

shifty See **underhand.**

shirk See **neglect.**

shiver See **shake.**

shocking See **unspeakable.**

shoddy 1. See **careless. 2.** See **cheap.**

short ***adj.*** **1. brief.**
SHORT describes what has little length (*a short skirt*), covers a small distance (*a short walk*), or takes a small amount of time (*a short trip*). BRIEF refers only to what is short in time or duration (*a brief period; a brief description*) or what is short in length (*a brief report; a brief letter*).
Antonym: **long.**

2. SHORT also applies to what has less than ordinary height: *a short, pudgy man.*
Antonym: **tall.**

shortage See **deficiency.**

shortcoming 1. See **disadvantage. 2.** See **weakness.**

show ***v.*** **display, exhibit, expose, reveal.**
All these verbs refer to presenting something to view. SHOW is the most general: *showed her the necklace; show goods in a store; a picture that shows a dinosaur.* DISPLAY usually suggests an attempt to present something to best advantage (*models displaying the latest fashion*), but it can imply ostentation (*displayed his wealth*) or even the making obvious of something better concealed (*ashamed to display his ignorance*). EXHIBIT suggests open, rather formal presentation that invites inspection: *an artist who exhibits his paintings at a gallery.* EXPOSE usually involves uncovering (*expose one's back to the sun*), bringing from concealment (*exposed the grain of the wood by cleaning*), or unmasking (*exposing a dishonest employee*). To REVEAL is often to disclose something that has hitherto been kept secret (*revealed her travel plans*).
Antonym: **hide.**

shrewd ***adj.*** **astute, quick-witted, sagacious.**
All of these adjectives refer to the possession of a keen, searching intelligence combined usually with sound judgment. SHREWD stresses perceptiveness, hardheadedness, cunning, and an intuitive knack in practical matters. SAGACIOUS emphasizes more profound wisdom and a gift for discernment and far-sightedness. ASTUTE suggests qualities associated with practical wisdom, such as acute understanding, insight, discernment, and immunity to being deceived. QUICK-WITTED, the narrowest term, refers to alertness and mental adroitness.

shrink See **contract.**

shudder See **shake.**

shun See **avoid.**

shy ***adj.*** **bashful, coy, diffident, modest.**
All of these describe persons who are fearful of intruding or being self-assertively brash. They can also apply to the behavior, actions, manner, etc., of such persons. SHY implies either a retiring or withdrawn nature (*a shy man who avoided parties*) or timidity resulting from lack of social experience (*a shy young girl*). BASHFUL suggests embarrassment or awkwardness in the presence of others: *They were too bashful to kiss good-by.* COY suggests false modesty or shyness designed to attract the interest of others: *a coy look.* DIFFIDENT implies lack of self-confidence: *diffident about making suggestions; a diffident greeting.* MODEST is associated with a retiring nature (*a modest and gentle woman*) and absence of vanity (*modest about his accomplishments*).
Antonym: **bold.**

shyness See **diffidence.**

sick ***adj.*** **ill, indisposed, unwell.**
These describe persons who are not in good physical or mental condition. SICK, ILL, and UNWELL are used interchangeably. INDISPOSED refers to minor sickness: *Although she was indisposed, the singer did not cancel her performance.*
Antonym: **healthy.**

sicken See **repel.**

sickening See **unspeakable.**

sidestep See **skirt.**

sign ***n.*** **badge, indication, mark, note, symptom, token.**
SIGN and its synonyms are compared as they denote outward evidence of something. SIGN, the most general, can refer to almost any such manifestation. A BADGE is usually something worn that shows rank, office, membership, condition, etc.: *Her mink coat was a badge of success.* MARK can refer to a personal characteristic or evidence of some quality or condition (*Intolerance is the mark of a bigot*); it can also denote evidence of an experience (*Poverty had left*

its mark on him). TOKEN usually refers to something that serves as a symbol, often of something intangible: *A white flag is a token of surrender.* INDICATION refers to evidence of a condition: *Dark clouds are often an indication of rain.* SYMPTOM frequently suggests visible evidence of an adverse condition: *Fever is a symptom of illness.* A NOTE is a characteristic or feature that reveals a certain quality: *a note of mysticism in his novels.*

significance See **meaning.**

significant See **important.**

signification See **meaning.**

silly See **foolish.**

simper See **smile.**

simple ***adj.*** **uncomplicated.**
SIMPLE and UNCOMPLICATED apply to what is not involved or complex. *Simple* can specifically describe what is not complicated in structure (*a simple microscope; a simple lens*) but also applies more generally (*a simple explanation; the simple truth*). *Uncomplicated* describes what is easy to understand or deal with: *an uncomplicated explanation; an uncomplicated jigsaw puzzle.* See also **easy; natural; plain; unintelligent.**
Antonym: **complex.**

simulate See **pretend.**

sincere See **true.**

single ***adj.*** **individual, separate, sole, solitary, unique.**
These adjectives refer in various ways to the condition of being one in number. SINGLE means "one only," that is, not in accompaniment or association or combination with another or others: *a single rose.* SOLE stresses the idea of "one and only," either in the sense of being the only one in existence or the only one involved in what is under consideration: *her sole purpose.* UNIQUE applies to what is the only one of its kind in existence: *Amassing a great fortune was his unique goal in life.* SOLITARY applies to what exists

alone (*a solitary traveler*) or to the condition of isolation (*solitary places*). INDIVIDUAL makes specific reference to one person or thing distinguished from the mass to which it belongs or from all others: *for each individual child; individual words*. SEPARATE, as compared here, implies the condition of being one and distinct by reason of being disunited from all others under consideration: *Libraries have a separate section for reference books*.

singular See **uncommon.**

size See **bulk.**

sizzling See **hot.**

skeleton See **draft.**

skepticism See **uncertainty.**

sketch See **draft.**

skid See **slide.**

skill See **ability.**

skinny See **thin.**

skirt *v.* **bypass, circumvent, hedge, sidestep.**
Core meaning: To evade, as a topic, by circumlocution (*skirted the serious questions*).

slack 1. See **loose. 2.** See **neglect.**

slacken See **relent.**

slam See **hit.**

slash See **lower.**

slavery See **bondage.**

sleek See **unctuous.**

slender See **thin.**

slice See **cut.**

slick See **glib.**

slide *v.* **coast, glide, skid, slip.**
SLIDE and its synonyms refer to moving smoothly and easily over or as if over a surface. *Slide* usually implies rapid and

easy movement without loss of contact with the surface: *slid the plate across the table.* SLIP more often is applied to accidental movement causing a fall, or threat of a fall, to the surface: *slipping on the ice.* GLIDE refers to smooth, free-flowing, and seemingly effortless movement: *glided his fingers along the strings of the instrument; a submarine gliding through the water.* COAST applies specifically to effortless movement due to gravity or inertia: *The car coasted to a stop.* SKID generally implies involuntary and uncontrolled movement with much friction: *The truck skidded on the slippery pavement.*

slim See **thin.**

slip See **slide.**

slipshod See **careless.**

sloppy 1. See **careless. 2.** See **disorderly.**

slow ***adj.*** **deliberate, dilatory, leisurely.**
All of these describe what acts, moves, happens, or is accomplished at a low speed. SLOW is the least specific: *slow traffic; a slow dance; slow motion.* DELIBERATE implies that lack of speed is related to careful consideration of every move or step: *a deliberate choice of words.* DILATORY implies such faults as delay and wasting time: *Your dilatory research has put us all behind schedule.* LEISURELY suggests lack of time pressure: *We took a leisurely tour of the islands.* See also **delay; dull.**
Antonym: **fast.**

slug See **hit.**

smack See **hit.**

small See **little.**

smart 1. See **clever. 2.** See **intelligent.**

smash See **hit.**

smile ***n.*** **grin, simper, smirk.**
SMILE and its synonyms denote facial expressions in which the mouth is curved upward slightly at the corners. *Smile* is the most general, since it can cover a wide range of feelings,

from affection to malice. A GRIN is a broad smile that exposes the teeth; usually it is a spontaneous expression of good humor, approval, or triumph. A SIMPER is a silly or self-conscious smile. A SMIRK is a knowing, simpering smile that often expresses derision or suggests smugness or conceit.

smirk See **smile.**

smooth See **level.**

snatch See **catch.**

sneaky See **underhand.**

soar See **rise.**

sober ***adj.*** **temperate.**
A person who is SOBER is not drunk. A TEMPERATE person exercises moderation and self-restraint and for that reason is unlikely to drink to excess.
Antonym: **drunk.**

sobriety See **abstinence.**

sociable See **social.**

social ***adj.*** **companionable, convivial, sociable.**
Core meaning: Characterized by or spent in the company of others (*a pleasant social afternoon*).

society 1. See **circle. 2.** See **union.**

sock See **hit.**

soften See **relent.**

soiled See **dirty.**

sole See **single.**

solid See **unanimous.**

solitary 1. See **alone. 2.** See **single.**

solitude ***n.*** **isolation, seclusion.**
SOLITUDE and its synonyms denote the state of being alone or of being withdrawn or remote from others. *Solitude* implies the absence of all other persons but is otherwise not

specific. ISOLATION can refer to the condition of one person, a group, or even a unit such as a country; in every case it emphasizes total separation from others. SECLUSION can apply to one person or a group and suggests being removed or apart from others though not necessarily completely inaccessible.

sophistic See **fallacious.**

sorrow ***n.*** **anguish, grief, heartache, regret, woe.**
These nouns relate to mental distress. SORROW connotes sadness caused by misfortune or loss; sometimes it suggests remorse for having done something: *sorrow at the illness of a friend; felt sorrow because she had treated her father with disrespect.* GRIEF is deep, acute personal sorrow resulting from irreplaceable loss: *Her death filled him with grief.* ANGUISH implies agonizing grief so painful as to be excruciating: *cries of anguish.* HEARTACHE is a feeling of sorrow that often implies longing for something out of reach: *heartache over his child's handicap.* REGRET ranges from suggesting mere disappointment (*a shrug of regret that their plans had not worked out*) to implying a painful sense of loss, bitterness, etc. (*deep regret over his failures*). WOE is intense, prolonged unhappiness or misery: *His isolation increased his woe.*
Antonym: **joy.**

sorrowful See **sad.**

sort See **type.**

sound 1. See **healthy. 2.** See **valid.**

source See **origin.**

spacious See **broad.**

species See **type.**

specific See **explicit.**

specious See **fallacious.**

spectral See **ghastly.**

speculation See **theory.**

speculative See **theoretical.**

speech ***n.*** **1. discourse, lecture, oration, talk.**
Core meaning: A formal oral communication to an audience (*a valedictory speech at graduation*).
2. See **language.**

speed See **expedite.**

speedy See **fast.**

spirit ***n.*** **brio, dash, élan, esprit, liveliness, pep** (*Informal*).
Core meaning: A lively, emphatic, eager quality or manner (*danced with great spirit*).

spiteful See **vindictive.**

splendid See **excellent.**

spoil See **pamper.**

spotless See **clean.**

spread ***v.*** **expand, extend, open, outstretch, unfold.**
Core meaning: To move or arrange so as to cover a larger area (*spread the blanket on the grass; a bird spreading its wings in flight*).

spur See **provoke.**

spurious See **fallacious.**

spurn See **reject.**

squabble See **argue.**

squander See **waste.**

square See **conventional.**

stale ***adj.*** **flat, tired.**
These describe what has lost its freshness or effectiveness through age or overuse. STALE has broad literal and figurative application: *stale crackers; stale ideas.* FLAT suggests a lack or loss of sparkle, either literal or metaphorical: *flat champagne; flat jokes.* TIRED refers to what is worn out (*tired outfits*) or hackneyed (*tired comments*).
Antonym: **fresh.**

stance See **posture.**

standard 1. See **ideal. 2.** See **normal.**

stare See **gaze.**

start See **begin.**

startle See **frighten.**

state 1. See **nation. 2.** See **say.**

stately See **grand.**

staunch See **faithful.**

stay See **stop.**

steadfast See **faithful.**

stealthy See **secret.**

step See **move.**

sterile See **barren.**

stern See **harsh.**

stick See **bond.**

stiff See **inflexible.**

still See **motionless.**

stimulant See **stimulus.**

stimulate See **provoke.**

stimulus ***n.*** **catalyst, impetus, impulse, incentive, motivation, stimulant.**
Core meaning: Something that causes and encourages a given response (*free enterprise as a stimulus to the economy*).

stingy ***adj.*** **close, miserly.**
These suggest reluctance to give or spend. STINGY is the most general; often it implies meanness of spirit as well as lack of generosity: *stingy with money and stingy with praise*. MISERLY suggests greed and hoarding: *too miserly to leave a tip*. CLOSE describes excessive and often annoying caution in money matters. See also **cheap.**
Antonym: **generous.**

stipend See **wage(s).**

stirring See **moving.**

stop *v.* **1. arrest, cease, check, discontinue, halt, stay.**
Core meaning: To prevent the occurrence or continuation of (*stopped the execution of the prisoner; told us to stop the noise*).
2. cease, desist, discontinue, halt, leave off, quit.
Core meaning: To come to a cessation (*snow that finally stopped; a guard who yelled for us to stop*).

story See **lie.**

stout See **fat.**

straight 1. See **direct. 2.** See **conventional.**

straightforward See **direct.**

strain See **effort.**

strange *adj.* **1. new, unaccustomed, unfamiliar.**
These describe what was previously unknown: *strange animals of the jungle; new information; unaccustomed difficulties; an unfamiliar face.*
Antonym: **familiar.**
2. bizarre, curious, eccentric, odd, peculiar, quaint, queer, unusual.
All of these describe persons or things that are notably out of the ordinary: *her strange appearance; a bizarre hat; a curious coincidence; an eccentric habit; an odd name; a peculiar point of view; a land full of sloths and other quaint animals; a queer expression on his face; an unusual dress.*
Antonym: **familiar.**

strength See **force.**

strike 1. See **affect. 2.** See **hit.**

strike out See **cancel.**

stringency See **severity.**

strip See **undress.**

stripe See **type.**

stubborn See **contrary.**

stuff See **matter.**

stupendous See **fabulous.**

stupid 1. See **dull. 2.** See **unintelligent.**

stupor See **daze.**

style See **fashion.**

subdued See **quiet.**

submissive ***adj.*** **compliant, obedient, passive.**

These adjectives describe what yields readily to the authority of another: *a submissive employee; a compliant pupil; an obedient servant. Passive* implies offering no resistance whatever: *a passive child who was attacked regularly by the neighborhood bully.*

Antonym: **rebellious.**

submit See **yield.**

subordinate ***adj.*** **dependent, secondary.**

These describe what has less power or importance than something else of its kind. SUBORDINATE, the most general, applies to rank, authority, position, etc. DEPENDENT suggests a relationship based on need: *A child is dependent on its parents for shelter.* SECONDARY refers to what is not primary: *an idea of secondary importance.*

Antonym: **dominant.**

subsequent See **later.**

subsidy See **bonus.**

subsistence See **living.**

substance 1. See **heart. 2.** See **matter.**

subvert See **sabotage.**

succeed ***v.*** **flourish, prosper, thrive.**

All of these denote success in a chosen activity or enterprise. SUCCEED focuses on accomplishing something desired or attempted: *She succeeded in swimming the Channel. Efforts to reach a cease-fire will succeed.* FLOURISH, PROSPER, and THRIVE suggest growth and progress: *Their marriage is flourishing. His business is prospering. She is thriving as a lawyer.*

Antonym: **fail.**

succinct See **concise.**

succumb See **yield.**

sufficient ***adj.*** **adequate, decent, enough, satisfactory.**
Core meaning: Being what is needed without being in excess (*sufficient fuel to complete the trip*).

suggest ***v.*** **hint, imply, insinuate, intimate.**
These verbs all refer to conveying thoughts or ideas indirectly. SUGGEST in this context usually refers to a process in which something is called to mind by an association of ideas or train of thought: *a cavern that suggests a cathedral.* IMPLY refers to something involved or suggested by logical necessity: *Life implies growth and death.* HINT refers to expression that is indirect but contains rather pointed clues: *Our hostess hinted that it was time to leave.* INTIMATE applies to veiled expression that may be the result of discretion or reserve: *He intimated that there was trouble ahead.* INSINUATE refers to conveying something, usually unpleasant, in a covert manner that suggests underhandedness: *Are you insinuating that I am dishonest?*

suggestion See **trace.**

suitable ***adj.*** **appropriate, apt, fit, fitting, proper.**
SUITABLE implies ability to meet requirements related to a particular need or to an occasion: *clothes suitable for everyday wear.* What is APPROPRIATE to a thing or for an occasion especially befits it, and what is APT is notably to the point: *appropriate remarks; an apt reply.* FIT in this sense refers to what is adapted to certain requirements or capable of measuring up to them: *tools fit for the job; fit for heavy duty.* FITTING suggests close agreement with a prevailing mood or spirit: *a fitting observance of the holiday.* PROPER describes what is harmonious, either by nature or because it observes reason, custom, propriety, etc.: *a proper setting for a monument; the proper way to hold a fork.*
Antonym: **unsuitable.**

suitableness See **qualification.**

sultry See **hot.**

summit See **climax.**

sum (up) See **add.**

super See **excellent.**

supercilious See **proud.**

supererogative See **gratuitous.**

supererogatory See **gratuitous.**

superficial See **shallow.**

superfluity See **excess.**

superintend See **administer.**

supple See **flexible.**

support See **living.**

supposition See **theory.**

surpass *v.* **exceed, excel, outdo, outshine, outstrip, pass, top, transcend.**
Core meaning: To be greater or better than (*a wheat crop that surpassed last year's by two million bushels*).

surplus See **excess.**

surprise See **ambush.**

surreptitious See **secret.**

surround *v.* **circle, compass, encircle, enclose, gird, hem in, ring.**
Core meaning: To shut in on all sides (*a city surrounded by suburbs*).

survey See **analysis.**

suspended See **hanging.**

suspension See **abeyance.**

suspicion 1. See **distrust. 2.** See **doubt. 3.** See **uncertainty.**

swaddle See **wrap.**

swat See **hit.**

swathe See **wrap.**

sway See **dispose.**

swear See **pledge.**

swell See **expand.**

sweltering See **hot.**

swift See **fast.**

symptom See **sign.**

synthetic See **artificial.**

system See **method.**

table *n.* **chart, tabulation.**
Core meaning: An orderly, columnar display of information (*a table of mortgage rates*).

tabulation See **table.**

tacit See **implicit.**

tactic See **move.**

tactless *adj.* **clumsy, impolitic, indelicate.**
Core meaning: Lacking sensitivity and skill in dealing with others (*tactless remarks*).

take in See **accept.**

take up See **accept.**

tale See **lie.**

talent See **ability.**

talk See **speech.**

tall See **high.**

tally See **add.**

tamper See **interfere.**

tardy See **late.**

taunt See **ridicule.**

tax See **charge.**

teach *v.* **drill, educate, instruct, train, tutor.**
All of these refer to imparting knowledge or skill. TEACH is the most widely applicable. INSTRUCT usually suggests

methodical direction in a specific subject or area: *instructing students in English literature*. EDUCATE is comprehensive and implies a wide area of learning, achieved either by experience or, more often, by formal instruction in many subjects: *It is the responsibility of a community to educate each child*. TUTOR usually refers to private instruction of one student or a small group: *tutors children in mathematics*. TRAIN generally implies concentration on particular skills intended to fit a person, or sometimes an animal, for a desired role: *training young men to be good citizens; a school that trains drivers*. DRILL implies instruction or training by continuous repetition: *drilled the girl in irregular verbs*.

tediousness See **monotony.**

tedium See **monotony.**

tell See **say.**

temperament See **disposition.**

temperamental See **capricious.**

temperance See **abstinence.**

temperate See **sober.**

temporary *adj.* **fleeting, momentary, provisional, transient, transitory.**

These refer to what lasts for a limited time only. TEMPORARY applies to what is meant to last either while regular conditions are interrupted or until definitive arrangements can be made: *a temporary secretary; a temporary state capital*. PROVISIONAL suggests a makeshift arrangement to meet an immediate need: *a provisional shelter*. FLEETING, MOMENTARY, and TRANSITORY describe what is of brief duration; *fleeting* adds a note of melancholy: *The joys of this earth are fleeting*. TRANSIENT usually refers to what remains only a short time: *the transient population of hotels*.

Antonym: **permanent.**

tempt See **seduce.**

tenable See **justifiable.**

tender See **offer.**

tentative See **conditional.**

terminal See **last.**

terminate See **end.**

terminology See **language.**

terrify See **frighten.**

terse See **concise.**

theorem See **law.**

theoretical ***adj.*** **abstract, academic, speculative.**
Core meaning: Concerned with or restricted to a theory (*a plan still in the theoretical stages*).

theory ***n.*** **1. hypothesis, supposition.**
Core meaning: A belief used as the basis for action (*the theory of progressive education*).
2. conjecture, speculation.
Core meaning: Abstract reasoning (*the theory that Bacon wrote the plays attributed to Shakespeare*).

thin ***adj.*** **bony, gaunt, lean, skinny, slender, slim.**
As they are compared, these adjectives share the meaning of having a lack of excess flesh. THIN is the most neutral: *a thin man.* GAUNT and BONY suggest an emaciated or haggard appearance: *a gaunt face; bony elbows.* LEAN suggests trimness and good muscle tone (*a lean and agile cat*); SLENDER and SLIM often suggest elegance: *a slender* (or *slim*) *model.* SKINNY describes what is very thin: *skinny legs.*
Antonym: **fat.**

thorough See **utter.**

threaten ***v.*** **intimidate, menace.**
THREATEN and its synonyms refer to foretelling danger, promising evil or injury, or inspiring fear. *Threaten,* the most widely applicable, can refer to verbal promise of harm (*threatening the prisoners with physical punishment*), to forewarning (*Dark skies threaten rain*), or to having a character that puts someone or something in danger (*Landslides

threatened the mountain village). MENACE is limited principally to the last of the foregoing senses: *an oil slick that menaced the shoreline of California*. INTIMIDATE refers to inspiring fear in and often to inhibiting a person by a show or promise of force: *His pounding the table and shouting failed to intimidate the witness*.

thrifty See **economical.**

thrive See **succeed.**

tidy See **neat.**

tie *v.* **bind.**

TIE and BIND can often be used interchangeably when they literally mean to fasten or secure: *tie up a parcel; bind sheaves of grain together*. Figuratively *tie* sometimes implies confinement or restraint: *tied to his family because he was dependent on them; tied to his job because he was ambitious*. *Bind,* more strongly than *tie*, suggests bringing together positively or uniting: *Mutual interests often bind two people*.

Antonym: **untie.**

tight *adj.* **taut, tense.**

When they refer to what is literally drawn out to its fullest extent, TIGHT and TAUT can often be used interchangeably: *a tight* (or *taut*) *string*. *Tight* frequently suggests constriction or binding (*tight lips; tight shoes*). *Taut* implies strain (*a rope so taut it nearly broke; a taut and angry face*). TENSE describes what is stretched tight, often excessively tight (*tense muscles*), and to persons in a state of mental or nervous strain (*tense and anxious before the interview*).

Antonym: **loose.**

time(s) See **age.**

timid *adj.* **timorous.**

Both TIMID and TIMOROUS refer to persons who lack courage, boldness, or daring and therefore shrink from dangerous or difficult circumstances: *too timid to learn to swim; a timorous man who never asserted himself*. They can also apply to the behavior, actions, manner, etc., of those who are thus

easily frightened: *a timid expression on her face; a timorous attempt to explain why he did it.*
Antonym: **bold.**

timidity See **diffidence.**

timorous See **timid.**

tinker See **fiddle.**

tiny See **little.**

tipsy See **drunk.**

tirade *n.* **diatribe, harangue, jeremiad, obloquy.**
Core meaning: A long, violent, or blustering speech, usually of censure or denunciation (*went off on a tirade about the evils of big government*).

tire See **bore.**

tired See **stale.**

title See **name.**

toil See **work.**

token See **sign.**

tongue See **language.**

tool *n.* **implement, instrument, utensil.**
Core meaning: A device used to do work or perform a task (*carpentry tools*).

top See **surpass.**

topflight See **excellent.**

topnotch See **excellent.**

topple See **overthrow.**

torment See **afflict.**

torrid See **hot.**

torture See **afflict.**

total 1. See **utter.** 2. See **add.**

totalitarian See **absolute.**

touch 1. See **affect.** 2. See **trace.**

touching See **moving.**

towering See **high.**

toy See **fiddle.**

trace ***n.*** **dash, hint, shade, suggestion, touch.**
Core meaning: A barely perceivable indication of something (*not a trace of wrongdoing*).

trade See **business.**

traditional See **conventional.**

traffic See **business.**

train See **teach.**

trance See **daze.**

tranquil See **calm.**

tranquillity ***n.*** **calm, peace, serenity.**
In the sense in which they are compared, these nouns all indicate freedom from agitation, anxiety, or worry: *a feeling of tranquillity; sat down with deceptive calm; a little peace and quiet; the serenity that comes from solving a personal dilemma.*
Antonym: **anxiety.**

transcend See **surpass.**

transform See **change.**

transgression See **breach.**

transient See **temporary.**

transitory See **temporary.**

transmit See **send.**

transpose See **reverse.**

treacherous 1. See **faithless.** **2.** See **false.**

treasure See **appreciate.**

tremble See **shake.**

trespass See **breach.**

trice See **moment.**

trifle See **fiddle.**

trim See **neat.**

triumph See **victory.**

troublesome See **difficult.**

true *adj.* **1. accurate, correct, right.**
These describe what is free from error or consistent with fact, reason, or reality: *a true statement; an accurate reading; correct calculations; the right answer.*
Antonym: **false.**
2. genuine, honest, sincere.
All of these refer to what is free from hypocrisy or not calculated to mislead: *true concern; genuine enthusiasm; an honest response; a sincere apology.*
Antonym: **false.**
3. constant, faithful, loyal.
These terms apply to persons who are firm and unchanging in attachment to a person, cause, etc.: *a true friend; a constant admirer; a faithful wife; loyal servants of the government.*
Antonym: **false.**
4. See **authentic.**

trust *n.* **confidence, faith.**

trustworthy See **reliable.**

truth See **veracity.**
These all denote a firm belief that something is true, reliable, etc.: *Put your trust in God. She won my confidence by keeping her word. He had faith in his own ability to drive.* See also **confidence.**
Antonym: **distrust.**

tumble See **overthrow.**

tutor See **teach.**

twit See **ridicule.**

twofold See **double.**

type *n.* **breed, ilk, kind, sort, species, stripe, type, variety.**
Core meaning: A class that is defined by the common attribute or attributes possessed by all its members (*the type of person who gets angry easily*).

typical 1. See **characteristic. 2.** See **normal.**

tyrannical See **absolute.**

ugly *adj.* **hideous, unsightly.**
These apply primarily to what is displeasing to the eye: *an ugly face; a hideous gash; an unsightly scar. Ugly* and *hideous,* the stronger term, can also describe what is emotionally, morally, or otherwise offensive: *the ugly details of the argument; a hideous murder; a hideous accident; a hideous miscarriage of justice.*
Antonym: **beautiful.**

ultimate See **last.**

umpire See **judge.**

unable *adj.* **incapable, incompetent.**
UNABLE and INCAPABLE, when they follow a verb like *be,* denote inability to serve in a given function or to do something but do not necessarily reflect a negative judgment: *She was unable to type. He was incapable of learning physics.* INCOMPETENT implies actual failure: *an incompetent dentist.*

unaccustomed See **strange.**

unaffected See **natural.**

unalterable See **irrevocable.**

unanimous *adj.* **concurrent, solid.**
Core meaning: Being in or characterized by complete agreement (*a unanimous decision*).

unattainable See **impossible.**

unaware *adj.* **unconscious.**
These share the meaning of being beyond knowledge or cognizance. UNAWARE often suggests that something is escaping one's notice: *unaware of her departure.* UNCONSCIOUS can describe anything from a suppressed emotion

(*unconscious rage*) to total lack of awareness (*so involved in the discussion that he was unconscious of the storm outside*).
Antonym: **aware.**

unbelievable 1. See **fabulous. 2.** See **implausible.**

uncalled-for See **gratuitous.**

uncertainty ***n.*** **doubt, skepticism, suspicion.**
These all involve the condition of being unsure about something or someone. UNCERTAINTY and DOUBT usually imply a questioning state of mind (*uncertainty about taking the trip; has doubts about the accuracy of the report*). SKEPTICISM suggests in addition a doubting state of mind that requires proof: *skepticism about his friend's motives.* SUSPICION implies resistance to belief or acceptance, more from lack of trust than from tentativeness of feelings: *a suspicion that the cashier was stealing.*
Antonyms: **certainty; confidence.**

uncivil See **disrespectful.**

unclean See **impure.**

uncommon ***adj.*** **extraordinary, rare, singular, unique.**
UNCOMMON and its synonyms describe what is not usual or ordinary. *Uncommon* applies to what is not customary, a daily occurrence, widely used, or generally known: *an uncommon problem; uncommon abilities.* What is EXTRAORDINARY is very unusual or remarkable: *an extraordinary event.* RARE indicates that something occurs infrequently (*a rare disease*) or is highly valued (*a rare jewel*). SINGULAR suggests that something is extremely uncommon (*a singular ability to predict the future*) or very strange (*a singular decision to eat only eggs*). UNIQUE implies that something is one of a kind: *Things are either unique or not unique—they do not have to be unique to be uncommon.*
Antonym: **common.**

uncomplicated See **simple.**

unconscious See **unaware.**

unconventional *adj.* **atypical, novel, offbeat, unusual.**
Core meaning: Not usual or ordinary (*unconventional business methods; unconventional dress*).

unctuous *adj.* **fulsome, oily, sleek.**
Core meaning: Affectedly and self-servingly earnest (*The candidate had an oozing, unctuous manner*).

undependable See **unreliable.**

underhand *adj.* **1. devious, disingenuous, duplicitous, guileful, shifty, sneaky, underhanded.**
Core meaning: Marked by treachery or deceit (*underhand business practices*).
2. See **secret.**

underhanded See **underhand.**

underlying See **radical.**

undermine See **sabotage.**

understand See **comprehend.**

undoubted See **authentic.**

undress *v.* **disrobe, strip.**
UNDRESS, DISROBE, and STRIP denote removing clothes. *Undress* is the most neutral: *I undressed the children for bed. She undressed and ran a bath. Disrobe* is a more formal term: *The doctor asked the patient to disrobe. Strip* involves the removal of all clothing: *The guards stripped the prisoners in a search for concealed drugs. The athlete stripped and showered.*
Antonym: **dress.**

uneducated See **ignorant.**

unethical See **immoral.**

unfair *adj.* **inequitable, unjust.**
These all describe persons, thoughts, or deeds that fail to show proper and due consideration for all parties or factors

concerned in a matter. UNFAIR applies most widely. INEQUITABLE, a more formal term, implies partiality. What is UNJUST violates principles of law and ethics.
Antonym: **fair.**

unfaithful See **false.**

unfamiliar See **strange.**

unfasten See **detach.**

unfavorable ***adj.*** **adverse.**
Both of these describe what is disadvantageous or exerts an opposing influence and points to misfortune or an unsuccessful outcome. UNFAVORABLE has the wider application: *unfavorable working conditions; an unfavorable progress report; an unfavorable spot to grow roses.* ADVERSE sometimes implies hostility and opposition (*adverse criticism*) and sometimes merely describes what works against one's interest or welfare (*adverse circumstances*).
Antonym: **favorable.**

unfeasible See **impossible.**

unfit See **unsuitable.**

unfitting See **unsuitable.**

unfortunate ***adj.*** **unhappy, unlucky.**
UNFORTUNATE and the less formal UNLUCKY can be used interchangeably to refer to what meets with or brings undeserved misfortune: *an unfortunate* (or *unlucky*) *businessman; an unfortunate* (or *unlucky*) *investment.* UNHAPPY, which in this sense stresses that something is unfavorable, is rarely used to describe persons: *made a wrong decision in an unhappy moment; an unhappy outcome.*
Antonym: **fortunate.**

unfriendly ***adj.*** **antagonistic, hostile.**
UNFRIENDLY denotes the absence of friendliness; it often describes what is merely unpleasant or disagreeable (*unfriendly replies*) but can also imply stronger feelings of hostility (*an unfriendly nation*). ANTAGONISTIC suggests active

unfriendliness (*an antagonistic attitude*) and often implies contention or opposition (*During the cross-examination the prosecutor and the witness grew openly antagonistic*). HOSTILE describes what shows unfriendliness (*a hostile colleague*), enmity (*hostile troops*), or opposition (*hostile to the suggestion*).
Antonym: **friendly.**

unfruitful See **barren.**

ungainly See **awkward.**

unhappy 1. See **sad. 2.** See **unfortunate.**

unification *n.* coalition, consolidation, union, unity.
Core meaning: A bringing together into a whole (*a large country resulting from the unification of many small city-states*).

unimportant *adj.* inconsequential, insignificant.
These describe what has little or no value or importance: *an unimportant message; an inconsequential decision; an insignificant writer.*
Antonym: **important.**

unintelligent *adj.* simple, stupid.
These three apply to what has or shows little intelligence. UNINTELLIGENT is the most general term: *an unintelligent boy; an unintelligent answer.* SIMPLE can suggest not only lack of intelligence but also lack of sense: *a simple man who was easily cheated.* STUPID occasionally refers to a temporary state of mental dullness; it also applies to individual acts that are extremely foolish: *The class seemed a bit stupid today. Swallowing goldfish is a stupid way to spend your time.*
Antonym: **intelligent.**

uninterested *adj.* incurious, indifferent.
These are compared as they indicate a lack of interest or curiosity. UNINTERESTED and INDIFFERENT simply denote such absence. INCURIOUS is the most specific, implying a lack of both normal and intellectual curiosity.
Antonym: **curious.**

union ***n.*** **1. association, club, confederation, congress, federation, fellowship, league, order, organization, society.**
Core meaning: A group united in a common activity, interest, or purpose (*a trade union; a union of anti-war activists*).
2. See **unification.**

unique 1. See **single. 2.** See **uncommon.**

unite See **join.**

unity See **unification.**

universal See **law.**

universe ***n.*** **cosmos, creation, macrocosm, nature, world.**
Core meaning: The totality of all existing things (*man's continual quest to understand the universe*).

unjust See **unfair.**

unknown See **obscure.**

unlawful See **illegal.**

unlikely ***adj.*** **improbable.**
UNLIKELY and IMPROBABLE refer to what shows little or no likelihood of being true or of happening: *an unlikely story; an improbable alibi. Snow seems unlikely* (or *improbable*) *today.*
Antonym: **likely.**

unlucky See **unfortunate.**

unmannerly See **impolite.**

unmistakable See **clear.**

unmitigated See **utter.**

unnecessary ***adj.*** **inessential, needless, nonessential, unneeded.**
Core meaning: Not necessary (*used unnecessary force; unnecessary expenditures*).

unneeded See **unnecessary.**

unobtrusive See **quiet.**

unpleasant *adj.* **disagreeable, objectionable.**
UNPLEASANT and DISAGREEABLE describe what is offensive or fails to give pleasure or satisfaction: *an unpleasant, ill-tempered cab driver; an unpleasant confrontation between labor and management; a vain, disagreeable executive; a strong, disagreeable odor.* OBJECTIONABLE, a stronger term, implies that something is so offensive that it causes or is apt to cause protest: *objectionable language; a point of view that is objectionable to all parties in the dispute.*
Antonym: **pleasant.**

unpredictable See **capricious.**

unprincipled See **immoral.**

unprogressive See **reactionary.**

unqualified See **utter.**

unrealistic See **idealistic.**

unrealizable See **impossible.**

unreasonable *adj.* **illogical, irrational, unreasoned.**
Core meaning: Not governed by or predicated on reason (*unreasonable expectations; an unreasonable demand*).

unreasoned See **unreasonable.**

unreliable *adj.* **undependable, untrustworthy.**
These words describe persons and things that do not merit faith and confidence: *an unreliable acquaintance; an undependable old car; an untrustworthy opponent.*
Antonym: **reliable.**

unscrupulous See **immoral.**

unselfish *adj.* **selfless.**
UNSELFISH and SELFLESS can be used interchangeably to describe those who are without concern for themselves.
Antonym: **selfish.**

unsightly See **ugly.**

unspeakable *adj.* **1. indescribable, unutterable.**
Core meaning: That cannot be described (*unspeakable happiness*).

2. abominable, frightful, revolting, shocking, sickening.
Core meaning: Too awful to be described (*unspeakable acts of genocide*).

unsteadiness See **instability.**

unsuitable *adj.* **improper, inappropriate, inapt, unfit, unfitting.**
All of these can be used interchangeably to refer to what does not meet the requirements related to a particular need or occasion.
Antonym: **suitable.**

unthinkable See **impossible.**

untidy See **disorderly.**

untrustworthy See **unreliable.**

untruth See **lie.**

untruthfulness See **dishonesty.**

unusual 1. See **strange. 2.** See **unconventional.**

unutterable See **unspeakable.**

unwell See **sick.**

unworkable See **impossible.**

upbraid See **scold.**

update See **modernize.**

uprising See **rebellion.**

upset *adj.* **desperate, distraught, frantic, nervous.**
These apply to what shows mental or emotional disturbance. Upset is the most general: *an upset man who had lost his briefcase.* Desperate has the additional sense of a feeling of despair and hopelessness: *a desperate appeal for help.* Distraught suggests anxiety that makes concentration difficult: *distraught because of her son's death.* Frantic implies extreme agitation bordering on frenzy: *a frantic scream.* Nervous can describe moods ranging from mere unease to severe apprehension: *nervous about being late; so nervous he had to take a sedative.*
Antonym: **calm.**

urge *v.* **coax, exhort, plead, press.**
URGE and its synonyms refer to requesting or persuading a person to do something that one advocates. *Urge* suggests making an earnest appeal for such action: *urged her friend to accept the job; urging the passage of new laws to combat crime*. PRESS implies a more forceful and insistent attempt to persuade: *Joy pressed her aunt to stay for the weekend*. EXHORT suggests a strong or stirring appeal (*The preacher exhorted the congregation to repent*); PLEAD, a humble but fervent one (*His mother pled with him not to leave*); and COAX, an attempt to persuade through persistent use of courtesy, flattery, etc. (*coaxing the child to take her medicine*). See also **encourage.**

used See **old.**

useful See **practical.**

usual See **familiar.**

utensil See **tool.**

utopian See **idealistic.**

utter **1.** *adj.* **all-out, complete, consummate, outright, thorough, total, unmitigated, unqualified.**
Core meaning: Completely such, without qualification or exception (*an utter fool; utter chaos; had utter confidence in them*).
2. See **say.**

vacant See **empty.**

vacillate See **hesitate.**

vague *adj.* **hazy, indefinite, indistinct.**
These all apply to what is unclear to the eye, ear, or mind. VAGUE, the most general, basically indicates a lack of definite form: *a vague outline of a tree; vague sounds; a vague statement of goals*. HAZY applies to what is indistinctly felt, understood, or recalled: *a hazy recollection of the incident*. INDEFINITE refers to what lacks clarity or is unclearly expressed: *an indefinite statement of purpose*. INDISTINCT suggests what is ill defined and lacks shape,

form, or character: *an indistinct footprint*. See also **ambiguous.**
Antonym: **clear.**

valiant See **brave.**

valid *adj.* **conclusive, convincing, sound.**
These apply to statements, arguments, and reasoning; they greatly heighten the effectiveness or force of what they describe. VALID and SOUND apply to what can be shown to be in accord with fact, truth, right, common sense, or legal force, and therefore is able to resist challenge or attack: *a valid objection; a valid passport; a sound case; sound title to the property*. CONVINCING applies to what is persuasive, even though it may not in fact be true: *His presentation is very convincing, but his evidence is suspicious*. What is CONCLUSIVE is decisive and thus capable of putting an end to doubt or debate: *a conclusive argument*.
Antonym: **invalid.**

valuable *adj.* **inestimable, invaluable, precious, priceless.**
Core meaning: Of great value (*valuable Elizabethan manuscripts*).

value See **appreciate.**

vanished *adj.* **dead, defunct, extinct, lost.**
Core meaning: No longer in use, force, or operation (*vanished languages of ancient peoples*).

variety *n.* **1. diversity, heterogeneity, multifariousness, multiformity, multiplicity, variousness.**
Core meaning: The quality of being made of many different forms, kinds, or individuals (*lives a life of great variety; the incredible variety of cultural expression in New York*).
2. See **type.**

variousness See **variety.**

vary See **change.**

vaunt See **boast.**

vend See **sell.**

venerable See **old.**

veneration See **honor.**

vengeful See **vindictive.**

venomous See **malevolent.**

vent See **say.**

veracity *n.* **1. accuracy, correctness, exactitude, fidelity, truth.**
Core meaning: Correspondence with facts or truth (*trusted in the veracity of her report*).
2. See **honesty.**

verbosity See **wordiness.**

vernacular See **language.**

vertical *adj.* **perpendicular.**
VERTICAL and PERPENDICULAR refer to what is at right angles—or approximately so—to the plane of the horizon or of a supporting surface: *a vertical takeoff; the vertical walls of an apartment; the perpendicular side of a building.*
Antonym: **horizontal.**

vex See **annoy.**

vice *n.* **corruption, depravity, immorality, wickedness.**
These all denote serious moral failings. VICE is the most general; it can refer to a moral flaw or weakness that inclines a person to evil or, in a weaker sense, to any defect of character: *Vice is not hereditary. Some people consider smoking a vice.* CORRUPTION connotes lack of moral restraint (*corruption in the court of the aging emperor*) or dishonesty or improper behavior, often by persons in positions of authority (*corruption at city hall*). DEPRAVITY suggests moral debasement: *a molester of children whose depravity was obvious to his fellow prisoners.* IMMORALITY in this sense often suggests extreme indulgence in sensual pleasures. WICKEDNESS implies viciousness.
Antonym: **virtue.**

vicious See **cruel.**

victory *n.* **conquest, triumph.**
These refer to the fact of winning, in war or in a competition. VICTORY, the general term, is broadly interchangeable

with the others but lacks their overtones. CONQUEST connotes physically forcing an enemy nation to submit; it can also refer to overcoming barriers of other sorts, as to understanding or control: *the conquest of yellow fever.* TRIUMPH refers to a victory or success that is noteworthy because it is decisive, significant, or spectacular: *Caesar's triumph in Gaul; a role that was the triumph of the actor's career.*
Antonym: **defeat.**

view ***n.*** **1. outlook, perspective, prospect.**
Core meaning: An evaluation or prediction about something (*curious about her views on the upcoming contract negotiations*).
2. See **opinion.**

vigilant See **alert.**

vigorous See **active.**

vindicate ***v.*** **absolve, acquit, exonerate.**
This group shares the common meaning of demonstrating innocence of guilt or blame. To VINDICATE is to clear with supporting proof. To ABSOLVE is to clear of blame or guilt. To ACQUIT suggests a judicial decision in answer to a specific formal charge. To EXONERATE is to declare blameless.
Antonym: **accuse.**

vindictive ***adj.*** **revengeful, spiteful, vengeful.**
Core meaning: Disposed to seek revenge (*a bitter, vindictive person*).

violation See **breach.**

violence See **force.**

virile See **male.**

virtue ***n.*** **goodness, morality, righteousness.**
All of these denote moral excellence. VIRTUE, MORALITY, and RIGHTEOUSNESS suggest conformity to standards of what is right and just or to approved codes of behavior; all imply uprightness: *Virtue is its own reward. The newspaper ques-*

tioned the morality of supplying weapons to both sides in the foreign uprising. They were convinced of the righteousness of their cause. GOODNESS often connotes inherent qualities of kindness, benevolence, or generosity: *Goodness and honesty showed in his every action.*
Antonym: **vice.**

virtuous See **moral.**

visionary See **idealistic.**

vital See **necessary.**

vituperative See **abusive.**

vivid See **graphic.**

vogue See **fashion.**

voice See **say.**

void See **invalid.**

volatile See **capricious.**

volume See **bulk.**

voluntary ***adj.*** **deliberate, intentional, willful.**
These four describe actions that are subject to control by the will of an individual. VOLUNTARY is the most general; it implies the exercise of free will (*a voluntary contribution to the pension fund*) or of choice (*living in voluntary exile*). DELIBERATE suggests what is done or said on purpose: *a deliberate theft.* INTENTIONAL further implies action that is undertaken for a specific purpose: *intentional insolence.* What is WILLFUL is said or done in accordance with one's own will and often suggests obstinacy: *a willful waste of time; willful disobedience.* See also **intentional; optional.**
Antonym: **involuntary.**

voracious ***adj.*** **avid, omnivorous, rapacious, ravenous.**
Core meaning: Having an insatiable appetite for an activity or pursuit (*a voracious reader*).

vow See **pledge.**

vulgar See **coarse.**

wage(s) ***n.*** **earnings, emolument, fee, pay, salary, stipend.**
Core meaning: Payment for work done (*an hourly wage of $8.50*).

wallop See **hit.**

wanton See **gratuitous.**

wares See **goods.**

warning ***n.*** **admonishment, admonition, caution, caveat, forewarning.**
Core meaning: Advice to beware of a person or thing (*disregarded his friend's warnings*).

wary See **alert.**

waste ***v.*** **consume, deplete, dissipate, drain, exhaust, expend, fritter, squander.**
These refer to the unwise or needless use of money, time, energy, or any kind of supply. WASTE is the least specific: *wasted $100 on a new gadget that he didn't need; wastes hours watching television when he should be studying; wasting space.* CONSUME, DRAIN, EXHAUST, and EXPEND often suggest that something has been used up completely: *Haggling over the details consumed precious hours. The hectic life he led began to drain his resources. The diver exhausted his air supply. The rocket's fuel was expended rapidly when the auxiliary tank began to leak.* To DEPLETE is to reduce the amount of something until little or none remains: *Our oil supplies have been seriously depleted.* FRITTER (always used with *away*) also implies gradual reduction: *kept the boys from frittering away their time.* SQUANDER nearly always suggests extravagance: *squander money.* To DISSIPATE is to use up in an intemperate manner: *He dissipated his life's savings by gambling.*
Antonym: **save.**

wasted See **haggard.**

watchful See **alert.**

waver See **hesitate.**

way See **method.**

waylay See **ambush.**

weak See **implausible.**

weaken See **relent.**

weakness ***n.*** **failing, foible, frailty, infirmity, shortcoming.**
Core meaning: A liking or personal preference (*a weakness for chocolate*).

wealthy See **rich.**

weary See **bore.**

wedding See **marriage.**

wedlock See **marriage.**

weight See **charge.**

weighty **1.** See **heavy.** **2.** See **important.**

welcome **1.** See **pleasant.** **2.** See **accept.**

well See **healthy.**

whack See **hit.**

wicked See **malevolent.**

wickedness See **vice.**

wide See **broad.**

wield See **handle.**

will ***n.*** **decision, determination, resolution, resolve.**
Core meaning: The power to make choices and act upon them in spite of difficulty or opposition (*lacked the will to gamble on his plan*).

willful **1.** See **contrary.** **2.** See **voluntary.**

win See **earn.**

windiness See **wordiness.**

wise ***adj.*** **judicious, prudent, sage.**
These terms describe persons, ideas, deeds, etc., that have or show understanding of what is true, right, or lasting. WISE and SAGE both suggest sound judgment, knowledge,

and experience; *sage,* the stronger of the two terms, sometimes has connotations of veneration and is often applied to intellectuals: *a wise statesman; a wise decision; a sage philosopher; a sage remark.* JUDICIOUS suggests forethought and caution: *a more judicious use of natural resources; a judicious man who chose his career with his limitations in mind.* PRUDENT stresses good judgment and common sense: *a prudent woman; a prudent approach to budgeting.*
***Antonym:* unwise.**

wisecrack See **joke.**

wish *n.* craving, desire, longing.
WISH and DESIRE apply to any strong inclination for a particular thing: *a wish to go to Paris; a desire to see the Eiffel Tower.* CRAVING implies an eager or intense desire: *a craving for strawberries.* LONGING suggests a persistent yearning, often for something unattainable: *a longing to go home.*

wistful See **pensive.**

withdraw See **recede.**

withhold See **refrain.**

withstand *v.* combat, fight, oppose, resist.
These verbs all imply a struggle or effort to overcome, defeat, or destroy. RESIST suggests an active attempt to work against something (*People resist change; they resist with all their might*); it often implies a successful effort (*resisted temptation*). WITHSTAND always stresses successful resistance: *They withstood every attack.* COMBAT, FIGHT, and OPPOSE do not necessarily connote a favorable outcome: *drugs to combat infection; combat an enemy; fighting crime; guerrilla groups fighting in the mountains; oppose an enemy; oppose new legislation.*
***Antonym:* yield.**

witticism See **joke.**

wobble See **shake.**

woe See **sorrow.**

womanly See **female.**

wonderful See **fabulous.**

wondrous See **fabulous.**

wordiness ***n.*** **prolixity, verbosity, windiness.**
Core meaning: Words or the use of words in excess of those needed for clarity or precision (*obscured her meaning with wordiness*).

wording ***n.*** **diction, parlance, phraseology, phrasing.**
Core meaning: Choice of words and the way in which they are used (*the complex wording in a contract*).

work 1. ***n.*** **business, employment, job, occupation.**
These nouns apply specifically to what one does to earn a living. WORK is the most general; it can refer to the mere fact of employment (*looking for work*) or to a specified activity (*Her work was nursing*). A BUSINESS is the work or trade in which a person engages: *went into the detective business*. EMPLOYMENT and JOB both suggest activity in which a person is engaged and paid by another: *got regular employment at an airport; had a job in a bookstore*. An OCCUPATION as a means of making a living does not necessarily imply being employed by others: *Madame Curie was by occupation a chemist*.
2. ***n.*** **drudgery, labor, toil.**
These denote physical or mental effort to make or do something. WORK and LABOR are least specific: *at work in the field; put in hard work on writing his new book; the labor involved in planting a garden; the labor of correcting and grading papers*. DRUDGERY implies tedious or menial work: *household drudgery*. TOIL is strenuous and exhausting work.
3. ***v.*** See **operate.**

world See **universe.**

worn 1. See **haggard. 2.** See **old.**

worry See **anxiety.**

wrangle See **argue.**

wrap *v.* **enfold, envelop, invest, swaddle, swathe.**
Core meaning: To cover completely and closely, as with clothing (*wrapped the baby in a blanket*).

wrath See **anger.**

wretched See **sad.**

wrong 1. See **false. 2.** See **awry.**

yield 1. *v.* **bow, capitulate, defer, submit, succumb.**
These share the sense of giving in to what one can no longer oppose or resist. YIELD has the widest application: *yield to an enemy; yield to a superior argument; yielded when she saw it was hopeless.* BOW suggests giving in out of sheer necessity or out of respect for another: *bow to defeat; bow to greater expertise.* To CAPITULATE is to surrender under specified and stated conditions (*The Axis powers capitulated*); the word can also suggest surrender more generally (*capitulated to her demand for additional help*). DEFER implies giving way to superior authority or for reasons of courtesy: *I defer to your better judgment.* SUBMIT applies when one gives way out of necessity after offering resistance unsuccessfully: *They withstood the siege for months but submitted when their supplies gave out.* SUCCUMB strongly suggests submission to something overpowering or overwhelming: *succumbed to the pressures of society; succumbed to her desire for a candy bar.*
Antonym: **withstand.**
2. *n.* See **production.**
3. *v.* See **relent.**

yoke See **couple.**

young *adj.* **adolescent, juvenile, youthful.**
All of these apply to persons in the age group between childhood and adulthood. YOUNG and YOUTHFUL are the most general (*the young*—or *youthful—hero*); both can also suggest the freshness, vigor, appearance, etc., associated with youth (*young for her age; a youthful face*). ADOLES-

CENT and JUVENILE usually stress immaturity: *adolescent attitudes; juvenile behavior.*
Antonym: **old.**

youthful See **young.**

zeal See **passion.**

zenith See **climax.**

zone See **area.**

COLLECTIVE NOUNS

The words in the following list are collective, or group, terms—that is, names given to companies of animals, birds, or fish of the same kind. Each word is followed by an indication of the things that make up the group. When the word is also applied to human beings, that fact is noted and explained. The first seven words are basic ones, important to an understanding of the more special terms, which are arranged alphabetically and complete the listing.

brood Young offspring under the care of the same mother; especially, birds (fowl) or fish having a common birth. Or the word can be applied to the children of a single family.

drove Animals (most often cattle, sheep, swine, or geese) being driven as a body from one location to another. Less often, a large body of people moving or acting as one.

flight A group of birds or aircraft in flight together.

flock Sheep, goats, or other animals or birds (especially when on the ground) that live, feed, or travel together. Said of persons, the word usually means the congregation of a church or the followers of a single clergyman or leader in another sphere. Less formally, any large number of things, such as difficulties.

gang A company of wolves or wild dogs, or of buffalo or elk when herded. Applied to people, a company of young persons associating on a social basis; a band engaged in criminal or other unlawful pursuits; or a group of laborers on one job such as a construction project. Also, a set of matched tools.

herd	Cattle when tended by persons, or other animals such as antelope, elephants, zebras, and aquatic mammals such as whales and seals. The expression *the herd* refers to the multitude of common people regarded, unfavorably, as a mass of cattle.
pack	A band of wolves or dogs that run and hunt as a unit; less often birds, especially grouse. Or a band of persons, often engaged in criminal pursuits but sometimes associated as followers of a celebrity.
bevy	Animals, especially roe deer, or birds, particularly larks or quail. Or a group or assemblage of persons, often attractive girls or young women.
cast	Falcons or hawks, usually a pair, released by a falconer at one time.
cete	A company of badgers.
covert	A flock of coots.
covey	A family of partridges, grouse, or other game birds.
drift	A drove or herd, usually of pigs, hogs, or boars.
exaltation	A flight of larks.
fall	A group of animals born at one birth; also a covey of woodcock.
gaggle	A flock of geese.
gam	A herd of whales or a social gathering of whalers at sea.
kennel	A pack of dogs, especially hounds, usually housed in one place or under the same ownership.
kindle	A brood or litter, especially of kittens.
litter	Offspring produced at one birth by a mammal that bears more than one offspring at one time.

muster	A flock of peacocks.
nide	A nest or brood of pheasants.
pod	A large group of seals or whales.
pride	A company of lions.
rout	In much earlier usage, a company of people or animals, especially of knights or wolves.
school, shoal	A large group of aquatic animals, particularly fish, swimming together.
shrewdness	A company of apes.
skein	A flight of geese or other wildfowl.
skulk	In earlier usage, a band of stealthily moving creatures, especially of foxes.
sloth	A company of bears.
sord	A flight of mallards.
sounder	A herd of wild boar.
spring	A flock of teal.
stable	Horses (including racehorses) lodged in one place or under one ownership. Less often, a group of boxers under a single manager.
swarm	A large number of insects or other small organisms, especially when in motion; or a group of bees, with a queen bee, migrating to establish a new colony. Less often, a large number of persons or animals when moving in mass or in a disorderly fashion.
troop	Animals or birds, especially when on the move. Or a body of soldiers or other military personnel, or a unit of Boy Scouts or Girl Scouts.
warren	A colony of rabbits.
watch	A flock of nightingales.
wisp	A flock of birds, especially of snipe.

COLLATERAL ADJECTIVES

A collateral adjective is one that corresponds to a certain noun in meaning but not in form (appearance). The words are descended from different linguistic lines. For example, *cardiac* is the collateral adjective of *heart,* and *feline* of *cat*. The phrase *cardiac deficiency* indicates a heart ailment; *feline quickness* expresses a characteristic of cats. Collateral adjectives are especially useful to one who writes, but often are not readily accessible to the average writer. This is so because, in many cases, the adjectives are not everyday words and because their identity is not suggested by a corresponding noun.

The following list of collateral adjectives is not exhaustive but includes many of the more common ones. On each line the noun (the word known to the writer) appears first; following it is the corresponding adjective (the word sought). The list is arranged so that related pairs of terms are grouped together—those, for example, that apply to animals, those that name or describe parts of the body, and so on. The concluding portion of the list contains words that are unrelated.

Zoology

ant	formic; formican; myrmecoid
ape; monkey	simian
bat	chiropteran; chiropterous
bear	ursine
bee	apian
bird	avian
bird of prey	raptorial
bull	taurine
butterfly, moth, etc.	lepidopteral; lepidopteran; lepidopterous
cat	feline
cattle	bovine
chicken	gallinaceous; galline
cockroach	blattid
crab	cancrid; cancroid

crow; raven; rook	corvine
deer	cervine
dog	canine; cynoid
dragon	draconic
duck	anatine
eagle	aquiline
fish	piscine
flamingo	phoenicopteroid; phoenicopterous
flea	siphonapterous
fly, mosquito, etc.	dipteran; dipterous
fox	vulpine
frog	ranine; raninian
goat	capric; caprid; caprine; hircine
goose	anserine
hare; rabbit	leporid; leporine
hawk; falcon	accipitral; accipitrine
horse	equine; hippic
kangaroo; opposum	marsupial
lion	leonine
lizard	saurian
louse	pedicular
mite; tick	acarid
mole	talpid; talpoid
mouse; rat	muriform; murine
ostrich	struthionine; struthious
otter	lutrine
peacock	pavonian; pavonine
pig	porcine
pigeon	columbaceous; columbine
porpoise	phocaenid
sea horse	hippocampal; hippocampine
seal	phocacean; phocaceous; phocal; phocid; phocine
shark; ray	squalid; squaloid; selachian
sheep	ovine
skunk	mephitine

snake	ophidian
spider	arachnoid
squirrel	sciurid; sciuroid
swallow	hirundine; hirundinous
thrush	turdine; turdoid
tiger	tigrine
turtle, tortoise, etc.	chelonian; testudinal; testudinarious; testudinate
weasel, mink, etc.	mustelid; musteline
whale	cetacean; cetaceous
wolf	lupine
worm	annelid; annelidan; vermicular

Points of the Compass

east	oriental
north	boreal
south	austral
west	occidental

Parts of the Body

ankle	talar
arm	brachial
back	dorsal
belly	ventral
bladder	vesical
blood	hemal; hematic; hematoid
blood vessel	vascular
bone	osseous; osteal; osteoid
brain	cerebral
breast	mammary
buttocks	pygal
calf	sural
cheek	buccal
chest	pectoral; thoracic
chin	mental
ear	aural; otic

elbow	cubital
eye	ocular
eyebrow	superciliary
eyelash	ciliary
finger	digital
foot	pedal
forearm	cubital
forehead	frontal
gall bladder	cholecystic
gums	gingival
hair	capillary; pilar; pilary
hand	manual
head; skull	cephalic
heart	cardiac
heel	calcaneal; calcanean
hoof; nail; claw	ungual; ungular
joint	articular
kidney	nephric; nephritic; renal
knee	genual
leg	crural
lip	labial
liver	hepatic
loin	lumbar
lung	pulmonary
mouth	oral
neck	cervical; jugular; nuchal
nerve	neural
nose	nasal; rhinal
rib	costal
shoulder	scapular
side	sagittal
skin	cutaneous; dermal; dermic
skull	cranial
sole	plantar
spleen	lienal
stomach	gastric
tail	caudal
thigh	femoral

throat	faucial; jugular; pharyngeal
toe	digital
tongue	glossal; lingual
tooth	dental
vein	venous
wrist	carpal

Time

dawn	auroral
day	diurnal; quotidian
evening	vesperal; vespertinal; vespertine
hour	horal
month	mensal
morning	matutinal
night	nocturnal
week	hebdomadal; hebdomadary
year	annual

Seasons

fall	autumnal
spring	vernal
summer	aestival; estival
winter	brumal; hibernal; hiemal

Celestial Bodies

moon	lunar
star	astral; sidereal; stellar
sun	heliacal; solar

Family

brother	fraternal
daughter	filial
father	paternal
husband	marital
mother	maternal
nephew	nepotal; nepotic

sister	sororal
son	filial
uncle	avuncular
wife	uxorial

General

answer	respondent; responsive
apple	pomaceous
ashes	cinereous
atonement; expiation	piacular
author	auctorial
baldness	alopecic; glabrous
bank of a river or lake	riparian
barber	tonsorial
basis; foundation	fundamental
beard	barbate
beast	bestial
beauty	pulchritudinous
beginning	inchoate; incipient; initial
bell	tintinnabular; tintinnabulary; tintinnabulous
bishop	episcopal
blood; bloodshed	sanguineous
body	corporal; corporeal
boredom	tedious
brass	brazen
bristle	setaceous
bundle	fascicular; fasciculate
cave	spelean
chance	fortuitous
childhood; immaturity	puerile
church	ecclesiastical
circle; sphere	orbicular; orbiculate
city	metropolitan; urban
clay	argillaceous
commotion; disturbance	tumultuous
complaint	querulous
confusion; agitation	turbulent

contemplation	pensive
copper	cupreous; cupric; cupriferous; cuprous
cough	tussal; tussive
country	rustic
curve	sinuous
custom; habit	consuetudinary
dance	terpsichoreal; terpsichorean
danger	perilous
darkness	tenebrious; tenebrous
death	lethal; mortal; thanatoid
delay	cunctative
devil	diabolic; diabolical
diamond	adamantine
diligence	sedulous
drinking	bibulous
eagerness; sprightliness	alacritous
earthquake	seismic
egg	ovoid; ovoidal; ovular; ovulary
enemy; enmity	hostile
evil; infamy	nefarious
fear	pavid
feather	plumate; plumose
fever	febrile
field	campestral
fire	incendiary; igneous
flood	diluvial; diluvian
foam; froth	spumous; spumy
fold; crease; wrinkle	rugate; rugose
forest; tree	silvan; sylvan
form; shape; structure	morphic; morphologic; morphological
friendliness	amicable
fringe	fimbriate; fimbriated
frost	gelid
gambling	aleatory
gardening	horticultural

gardening, decorative	topiary
glass	vitreous; vitrescent
glue	glutinous
god	deific
gold	auric; auriferous; aurous
grain, especially wheat	frumentaceous
green	virid; viridescent
healthfulness	salubrious; salutary
heat	caloric; calorific; thermal; thermic
hiss	sibilant
honey	melliferous; mellific; mellifluous
hood; cowl	cucullate; cucullated
horn	corneous
hump; swelling	gibbous
hunger; starvation	famished
ice	glacial
impulsiveness	impetuous
indecency	obscene
indiscriminateness; immorality	promiscuous
indolence; futility	otiose
introduction; preliminary	prefatory
iron	ferric; ferriferous; ferrous; ferruginous
irritability; peevishness	petulant
island	insular
ivory	eburnean; eburneous
jumping; dancing	saltant; saltatorial; saltatory
kettle drum	tympanic
king; queen; monarch; ruler	regal; royal
kiss	osculatory
lake	lacustrine
land; earth	terrene; terrestrial
laugh	risible

law	jural; juridic; juridical; juristic; legal
laxity; negligence	remiss
leaf	foliaceous; foliar; foliate; foliose; frondescent, frondose
learning; knowledge	erudite
left	sinistral
legal proceedings; argumentation; debate	forensic
letter	epistolary
library	bibliothecal
life	vital
light	luminous; photic
love	amatory; amorous
marble	marmoreal; marmorean
marriage	hymeneal; marital; matrimonial
master; teacher, authority	magisterial
melancholy; gloom	morose
menace	minatorial; minatory
milk	lactary; lacteal; lactescent; lactic; lactiferous
model; specimen	exemplary
moisture	humid
money	financial; pecuniary
mother-of-pearl	nacreous
need	indigent
net; netting	reticular
notoriety	infamous
number	numeric; numerical
oak	quercine
oath	jurant; juratory
oceans or seas, open	pelagic
oil	oleaginous; unctuous
old age	senescent; senile

parish	parochial
pearl	margaric; margaritic
pleasure	hedonic; hedonistic
plunder	predaceous; predacious; predatory
pregnancy	gravid
priest	sacerdotal
probability; likelihood	verisimilar
prophesy	vaticinal
punishment	penal
rain	pluvial; pluvian; pluviose; pluvious
reason	rational
relentlessness	inexorable
resistance; disobedience	contumacious
resistance to motion, action, etc.	inert
right	dextral
ring	annular; annulate; annulated
river	fluvial
rudeness	contumelious
salt	saline
scale, as of fish	squamose; squamous; squamulose
school	academic
sea	marine; maritime
sewer	cloacal
shore; coast	littoral
shrub	frutescent; fruticose
silence	taciturn
silver	argent; argentine
sin; guilt	peccable; peccant
skin; film	pellicular
sky; heavens	celestial
slave; slavishness	servile
sleep	somnifacient; somniferous; somnific; somnolent
smell	olfactory

snow	nival
spontaneity	extemporaneous; extemporary; extempore
spot; stain	maculate
stone	lithic; petrous
stone, precious	lapidary
strap	ligulate
stubbornness	obstinate
stupidity; silliness	asinine; fatuous
sugar	saccharine
swamp	paludal
sweat	sudatory; sudorific
swimming	natant; natatorial; natatory
tailor; tailoring	sartorial
talkativeness	loquacious
taste	gustatory
tear	lachrymal
tenacity	pertinacious
tendency	prone
thorn	spinose; spinous
thrift	frugal
throat	guttural
tickle; agreeable excitement	titillative
time	chronological; temporal
touch	tactile
tree	arboreal; arboreous
trust	fiducial; fiduciary
twilight	crepuscular
universe	cosmic
walk	ambulant; ambulatory
wall	mural
wastefulness; extravagance	prodigal
water	aquatic
wax	ceraceous; cerated
wedge	cuneal; cuneate; cuneated; cuneiform

widow	vidual
wildness	feral
window	fenestrated
wing	alar; alate; alated
wink	nictitant; nictitating
whisper	susurrant; susurrous
whistle	sibilant
worthlessness; invalidity	nugatory
yawn	oscitant

SCIENCES AND TECHNOLOGY

Following are the names of some of the major sciences or branches of technology. Each name is preceded by a brief indication of its particular field of study and activity.

aircraft navigation	**aeronautics**
ancient life forms and fossils	**paleontology**
animals as an area of biological study	**zoology**
atmosphere, phenomena of the	**meteorology**
atomic and molecular systems, the composition, strucuture, properties, and reactions of	**chemistry**
bacteria, especially in relation to medicine and agriculture	**bacteriology**
biological substances and processes, chemistry of	**biochemistry**
birds, observation of as a branch of zoological study	**ornithology**
caves, the physical, geologic, and biological aspects of	**speleology**
celestial bodies	**astronomy**
cells, the formation, structure, and function of, considered as a branch of biology	**cytology**
charts and maps, the making of	**cartography**
drugs	
the composition, uses, and effects of	**pharmacology**
the preparation and dispensing of	**pharmacy**
earth, the	
and its features	**geography**
the mechanical properties of	**seismology**
the origin, history, and structure of	**geology**

earthquakes	**seismology**
electronic phenomena	**electronics**
energy and matter and the interaction between them	**physics**
environment, the relationship between organisms and their	**ecology**
fossils and ancient life forms	**paleontology**
heredity, the biology of	**genetics**
human beings, emergence of from earlier forms of life	**evolution**
insects, the world of	**entomology**
life and life processes	**biology**
life processes, activities, and functions, essential and characteristic, considered as a biological science	**physiology**
light and vision, the properties of	**optics**
living organisms	
the function, early growth, and development of	**embryology**
the structure, functioning, growth, origin, evolution, and distribution of	**biology**
existing outside the earth or its atmosphere, the biology of	**exobiology or astrobiology**
maps and charts, the making of	**cartography**
material systems, the action of forces on	**mechanics**
matter	
the composition, structure, properties, and reactions of	**chemistry**
the action of forces on	**mechanics**
and energy and the interactions between them	**physics**

mental processes and behavior	**psychology**
metals, the extraction of from their ores, the purification of, and the creation of useful objects from	**metallurgy**
minerals, the distribution, identification, and properties of	**mineralogy**
molecular and atomic systems, the composition, structure, properties, and reactions of	**chemistry**
mountains, including their physical geography	**orology**
nature, the constitution of	**cosmography**
nervous system, the, the structure and disorders of, considered as part of medical science	**neurology**
ocean, the, and its phenomena as an area of exploration and scientific study	**oceanography**
organisms	
and their environment, the relationship between	**ecology**
and their parts, the shape and structure of	**anatomy**
plant life, considered as a branch of biology	**botany**
radiation, the use of as a means of medical diagnosis and therapy and in the scientific examination of material structures	**radiology**
related groups of organisms, the historical development of	**evolution**
sound, the nature and properties of	**acoustics**
space flight	**astronautics**
tissue, animal and plant, anatomical study of the microscopic structure of	**histology**

universe, the	
evolution of	**cosmogony**
the origin, processes, and structure of	**cosmology**
beyond the earth	**astronomy**
upper atmosphere, the	**aeronomy**
vision and light, the properties of	**optics**
water, the properties, distribution, and effects of	**hydrology**
weather and weather conditions	**meteorology**

AFFIXES: WHAT THEY MEAN

a–

The basic meaning of the prefix *a–* is "without." For example, *achromatic* means "without color." Before vowels and sometimes *h, a–* becomes *an–*: *anaerobic*. Many of the words beginning with this prefix are used in science, such as *aphasia, anoxia,* and *aseptic*. It is important not to confuse *a–* with other prefixes, such as *ad–,* that begin with the letter *a*.

anti–

The prefix *anti–* goes back to Greek *anti,* meaning "against." *Anti–* is so recognizable and its meaning is so clear that it is frequently used to make up new words. For example, the meanings of words such as *anticrime* and *antipollution* are easy to guess. Sometimes, when followed by a vowel, *anti–* becomes *ant–*: *antacid*.

dis–

The prefix *dis–* has several senses, but its basic meaning is "not, not any." Thus *disbelieve* means "to refuse to believe" and *discomfort* means "a lack of comfort." *Dis–* came into English from the Old French prefix *des–,* which in turn came from the Latin prefix *dis–,* which came from the adverb *dis,* meaning "apart, asunder." *Dis–* is an important prefix that occurs very frequently in English in words such as *discredit, disrepair,* and *disrespect.*

hyper–

The basic meaning of the prefix *hyper–* is "excessive or excessively." For example, *hyperactive* means "highly or excessively active." *Hyper–* comes from the Greek prefix *huper–,* which comes from the preposition *huper,* meaning "over, beyond." *Hyper–* has been used actively in English since the 17th century and is now frequently used to make up new words, such as *hypercritical* and *hypersensitive.* In fact, most of the words in our language beginning with *hyper–* are relatively recent. Only a few, such as *hyperbole,* are of Greek origin.

hypo–

The prefix *hypo–* means "beneath, below, or under." It can be traced back to the Greek prefix *hupo–,* from the word *hupo,* meaning "beneath, under." A few English words, such as *hypocrite, hypocrisy,* and *hypochondria,* come from Greek words using *hupo–.* But most English words beginning with *hypo–* have been made up by scientists and physicians. *Hypo–* either means "below or under," as in *hypodermic,* or "less than normal," as in *hypoglycemia.*

inter–

The prefix *inter–* comes from the Latin prefix *inter–,* from the preposition *inter,* meaning "between, among." Thus the word *intercede,* in which *inter–* combines with the Latin verb *cedere,* "to go," means "to go between." Similarly, *interject,* which comes from Latin *iacere,* "to throw," means literally "to throw something between or among others." And *intervene,* coming from Latin *venire,* "to come," means "to come between people or things." In English, *inter–* is still producing new words, such as *interfaith, intertwine,* and *intercellular.*

mis–

The basic meaning of the prefix *mis–* is "bad; badly; wrong; wrongly." Thus *misfortune* means "bad fortune" and *misbehave* means "to behave badly." Likewise, a *misdeed* is "a wrong deed" and *misdo* means "to do wrongly." *Mis–* forms compounds primarily by attaching to verbs: *mishear, misremember. Mis–* also frequently forms compounds by attaching to nouns that come from verbs: *miscalculation, mismanagement, mispronunciation.* The prefix *mis–* can be traced back to Old English.

neo–

The prefix *neo–,* which comes from Greek, means "new or recent." Thus our word *neophyte,* which means "a recent convert" or "a beginner," comes from Greek *neophutos,* which meant literally "newly planted," from *neo–* plus *phutos,* "planted." Many words beginning with *neo–* do not come from Greek but have been formed in English over the last 150 years. Many of these words refer to a new or a modern form of a movement or doctrine, such as *neoconservatism* or *neofascism.* Many other relatively recent formations are science words, such as *neodymium.*

pre–

The basic meaning of the prefix *pre–* is "before." It comes from Latin *prae,* which means "before, in front." In fact, the word *prefix* comes from *prae* plus *fixus,* a form of the Latin verb *figere* ("to fasten"). *Pre–* often appears in combination with verbs of Latin origin. For example, as early as the 16th century we have *preconceive, preexist,* and *premeditate. Predispose* and *prepossess* came into use in the 17th century, and *prepay* came into use in the 19th century.

pro–

Pro– is a prefix that exists in two forms. The first comes from Latin *pro,* meaning "for." In English, this *pro–* usually means "favoring" or "supporting," as when it is prefixed to names of nationalities: *pro-American.* In this sense, the opposite of *pro–* would be *anti–: proslavery / antislavery.*

The other *pro–* comes from Greek *pro,* meaning "before, in front." The word *prologue* comes from Greek *prologos,* from *pro* plus *logos,* meaning "speech." In English, *pro–* often means "before" or "earlier" and is used mainly in science terms: *prophase.*

retro–

The prefix *retro–,* meaning "backward, back," comes from the Latin prefix *retro–,* meaning "backward, behind." The most common English words beginning with *retro–* are derived from Latin words or elements. *Retroactive* comes from Latin *retro–* and the verb *agere,* "to drive." *Retrograde* combines *retro–* with the verb *gradi,* "to walk." *Retrospect* adds *retro–* to the verb *specere,* "to look at." The 19th and 20th centuries have seen many scientific or technical terms coined with English *retro–,* such as *retrorocket.*

sub–

The prefix *sub–* can be traced back to the Latin preposition *sub,* meaning "under." Some words beginning with *sub–* that came into English from Latin include *submerge, suburb,* and *subvert.* When *sub–* is used to form words in English, it can mean "under" (*submarine, subsoil, subway*), "subordinate" (*subcommittee, subplot, subset*), or "less than completely" (*subhuman, substandard*). *Sub–* can form compounds by combining with verbs as well as with adjectives and nouns, as in *subdivide, sublease,* and *sublet.*

trans–

The prefix *trans–* goes back to the Latin prefix *trans–,* from the Latin preposition *trans,* meaning "across, beyond, through." Many of the most common English words beginning with *trans–* are derived from Latin words or elements, as in *transfer, transfuse, translate, transmit, transpire,* and *transport.* Another large group of words has *trans–* in combination with English adjectives, as in *transatlantic, transcontinental, transpacific,* and *transpolar,* with the meaning "across" or "through" a particular geographic element.